'Among the abundance of literature on lea
Monica Hanaway's unique contribution does
tential perspective on being a leader, capturi
cal depth that accompanies these positions
clear writing and to-the-point examples, ma:
thought into pragmatic solutions to common leadership ~~~~~~~
ing a vision or dealing with conflict, as well as discussing some of the most pertinent yet often un-addressed existential issues, which often weigh heavily on those
at the top. Becoming aware, managing and ultimately embracing the existential
challenges surrounding leadership will make the difference between those who
find themselves in a leading role and truly exceptional leaders ready to navigate
the unique challenges of the twenty-first century. A must read for everybody who
aspires to greatness and is eager to build the resilience needed to lead their people confidently into an uncertain future'. – **Yannick Jacob, positive existential
coach; trainer, supervisor and change agent; author of** *An Introduction to
Existential Coaching* **(Routledge, 2019)**

'Monica has delivered very popular workshops at Riga University. Her existential
psychological approach provides an interesting and valuable new way to approach
the challenges of leadership, coaching and conflict resolution. *An Existential
Approach to Leadership Challenges* shows how this philosophical approach can
be used effectively in approaching the challenges of leadership both strategic and
relational'. – **Ulla Zumente-Steele, Erasmus Institutional Coordinator, Riga
School of Law, Latvia**

'During my leadership and mediation training sessions in Guernsey with
Monica, she has demonstrated her application of existential thought and practice. Throughout these learnings, the dichotomy of existential versus traditional
leadership was explored, highlighting the importance of authenticity, values and
purpose in modern existential leadership styles, and the benefits of actively demonstrating the application of those attributes. As a leader, these studies have also
enabled me to approach coaching and conflict situations with a more acute self-
awareness and appreciate the impact of the individuals' outer world.

Monica illustrates the powers of the existential approach through brilliant
writing and real-life examples. I would encourage anyone to buy this book as a
resource and reference to those who are in, or who have a desire to be successful,
in a leadership role'. – **Chris Corbin, Head of Customer Service, First Central
Insurance and Technology Group, Guernsey**

'Monica has run trainings in Bucharest on her existential approach to business,
coaching and conflict resolution. It is good to see this approach detailed in her new
book *An Existential Approach to Leadership Challenges*. The book introduces
the core concepts of the existential approach and also shows, in a very practical
way, how this approach can be used in some of the main tasks of organisational
leadership. It shows that effective, mindful dialogue focused on existential concerns lies at the heart of good leadership'. – **Madalina Calcun, Department for
Open Government and Civil Society, Bucharest, Romania**

'All leaders will encounter challenges and many of these have the potential to cause conflict. In *An Existential Approach to Leadership Challenges*, Monica Hanaway demonstrates how to bring a philosophical approach into day-to-day leadership. Using her approach can help to reduce the number of workplace conflicts, but should conflicts occur, as they inevitably will, she offers existentially informed introductions to conflict coaching and mediation. This makes the book a valuable resource to leaders, but also to coaches and mediators'. – **Mugur Mitroi, President of Mediation Council of Romania**

'Successful leadership and management of any organization can only be achieved when the leader truly understands psychological aspects. Monica Hanaway perfectly outlines the most important theoretical and practical issues in her new book, helping the reader to discover the impact of psychology on leadership. Monica Hanaway's book *An Existential Approach to Leadership Challenges* is the key to each reader's next, successful career steps, which is only possible through nuanced understanding of psychology in leadership. Never before has an existential approach been explained so brightly. – **Dana Rone, advocate at law, accredited mediator; member of the Disciplinary Commission of Sworn Advocates in Latvia; lecturer at Turiba University, Riga, Latvia**

'This is an important book for existential leadership in the twenty-first century, where uncertainty is rarely acknowledged let alone expressed. To be certain is the name of the game in many circles where confidence and certainty often go hand in hand. Monica Hanaway addresses the challenges that existentialism brings – uncertainty, authenticity, relatedness, freedom and meaning making. She shows the reader why each of these "existentials" can be challenging for corporate leaders or for anyone who is responsible for managing others. She argues convincingly that understanding and embracing these existential challenges enhances and creates modern leaders who are equipped to deal with all the challenges that come with the role of leader. One everyday challenge is conflict. We are shown how conflict can be accepted and handled creatively or how an existential leader can prevent, manage or resolve conflict via coaching or mediation. I highly recommend this well-written practical book that is also full of common sense and wisdom'. – **Diana Mitchell, UKCP psychotherapist; accredited mediator; lecturer, Regent's University, London, UK**

'The emphasis in leadership is changing. The increasing pace of change and complexity calls for a different approach, meaning leaders must adapt their leadership style. *An Existential Approach to Leadership Challenges* builds on Monica Hanaway's previous book, giving concrete examples of how existential thought can help address common leadership challenges'. – **Felix Spender, former army officer, international negotiator and SME business leader**

'Monica Hanaway worked in Belfast and Cape Town with paramilitaries and township residents, for the Tutu Foundation UK. I was extremely impressed by Monica's disciplined psychologically informed way, not telling anyone what to do, or promising anything which couldn't be delivered. Her approach demonstrates the extraordinary parallels between Existential Phenomenology and the African philosophy and tool of Ubuntu, lived and promulgated by Desmond Tutu and indeed Nelson Mandela. All types of leaders can gain from the approach described in *An Existential Approach to Leadership Challenges*'. – **Clive Conway, Chair of the Tutu Foundation UK; Patron: Archbishop Desmond Tutu, Honorary Patron: FW de Klerk, London, UK**

'I first encountered Monica when she gave a presentation to the Lawyers Network. I then engaged her as a leadership coach to work with me in a time of transition when I was moving from a post I had held for many years to a new post in a very different sector. In her coaching she embodies the principles and practice she describes in *An Existential Approach to Leadership Challenges*. Her book presents a very clear explanation of existential leadership in action'. – **Mirjam Buyteweg, previous Global Head of Law, Sony Music; Head of Legal and Compliance, IFRS Foundation, London, UK**

'Uncertain times such as those we live in (and through) demand leaders who can engage with the challenges being provoked – be they personal, interpersonal or organisational. Monica Hanaway's wise and thought-provoking book *An Existential Approach to Leadership Challenges* succeeds in alerting and attuning today's leaders to the possibilities of leadership within a framework that does not seek to evade the uncertainties of living but rather attempts to delineate them so that they can be "worked with" rather than "fought against". Highly recommended'. – **Professor Ernesto Spinelli, author of *Practising Existential Therapy: The Relational World* (2nd Edition, 2015)**

An Existential Approach to Leadership Challenges

In *An Existential Approach to Leadership Challenges,* Monica Hanaway progresses us forward from a brief, introductory understanding of existential thought to considering how this approach can positively address the practical leadership challenges our twenty-first century leaders face today.

Hanaway presents a practical framework to tackle the greatest challenges in leadership, such as creating an inspiring and authentic vision, recruiting, retaining and developing staff and dealing with conflict. In Part I, she presents an overview of existential thought and what existentialism can bring to leadership, helping resolve issues of uncertainty, authenticity, relatedness, freedom and meaning making. In Part II, she explores how to work practically with an existential leadership approach, showing how existentialism can help communicate a vision, examining the vision statements of existing businesses as case studies and explaining the importance of this in recruiting, developing and retaining staff. Finally, she explores how the existential approach is beneficial in preventing, managing and dealing with conflict, defining what conflict is and introducing existentially informed conflict coaching and psychologically informed mediation practice. Combining philosophical and practical thinking, Hanaway has made existentialism an accessible resource for all leaders.

This book will appeal to future leaders in practice and in training, and anyone in a leadership role. It will also be of interest to academics and students of coaching and coaching psychology, as well as to those interested in applied philosophy and psychology.

Monica Hanaway is an executive and leadership coach, business consultant, mediator, psychotherapist and trainer. She is the author of *The Existential Leader* (Routledge) and runs training programmes on this approach. She is passionate in her mission to bring existential thought beyond the academic arena into the business world, believing it has much to offer leaders in these uncertain times.

An Existential Approach to Leadership Challenges

Monica Hanaway

Routledge
Taylor & Francis Group

LONDON AND NEW YORK

First published 2020
by Routledge
2 Park Square, Milton Park, Abingdon, Oxon OX14 4RN

and by Routledge
52 Vanderbilt Avenue, New York, NY 10017

Routledge is an imprint of the Taylor & Francis Group, an informa business

British Library Cataloguing-in-Publication Data
A catalogue record for this book is available from the British Library

Library of Congress Cataloging-in-Publication Data
A catalog record has been requested for this book

ISBN: 978-0-367-25183-3 (hbk)
ISBN: 978-0-367-25184-0 (pbk)
ISBN: 978-0-429-28641-4 (ebk)

Typeset in Times
by Nova Techset Private Limited, Bengaluru & Chennai, India

MIX
Paper from responsible sources
FSC
www.fsc.org   FSC® C013985

Printed in the United Kingdom
by Henry Ling Limited

Contents

Acknowledgements   xi

Introduction   1

Part I
What do we mean by 'existential leadership'?   5

1 What does it mean to be 'existential'?   7
   The four existential dimensions 12

2 What does it mean to be a leader?   15

3 The challenge of finding a new type of leadership
   for the 21st century   19

4 What challenges does existentialism bring to leadership?   25
   The existential challenges of leadership 25

Part II
Working practically with the existential leadership
approach   41

5 An existential approach to creating, communicating and
   implementing a vision   43
   An existential vision statement 47
   Using the existential components to create the vision 48
   Some value-led examples 49
   Communicating the vision: how to take your team with you 57

6 An existential approach to recruitment, retention and
  development of staff   61
  Using an existential approach in recruitment 61
  Using an existential approach in retaining staff 67
  *Using an existential approach in the development of staff (including
    an introduction to existential coaching and mediation) 74*
  What is the aim of existential coaching? 84
  Existential coaching and psychotherapy 86
  Models of existential coaching 89

7 An existential approach to preventing, managing
  and resolving conflict   113
  A psychological response to dealing with conflict 117
  Conflict coaching 128
  Mediation 131

  Conclusion   137
  Bibliography   139
  Index   147

Acknowledgements

I start with thanking my husband, who continues to offer support, encouragement, understanding and infinite patience. Without his quiet presence, I would not be able to take up many of the opportunities offered to me.

My daughters provide constant support and I am full of admiration and amazement for the way these two young women tackle this uncertain world with creativity. I thank them for being who they are.

I should like to thank those who have participated in my courses. Your questions help to develop my own thinking and your question, 'Is there somewhere where you have written this all down?' prompted the writing of this and my previous books.

My thanks also go to those companies who invite me in to work with their leadership groups. It is heartening to see the growth of interest in the existential approach across small businesses and charities, through to large global companies and organisations.

My two briard dogs, who lie either side of my desk as I type, also deserve a mention for their patient support and unflappability when technical mishaps occur and I lose what I have written and engage in emotional, verbal release! It is true that stroking dogs lowers the blood pressure.

Finally, I should also like to thank Diana and Allan Mitchell, who graciously allowed me to use one of their son, Duncan Mitchell's paintings as the starting point for the design for the book cover. I am pleased that they approved of my addition of a mosaic of existential challenges.

Introduction

My original intention in writing the previous book, *The Existential Leader – An Authentic Leader for Our Uncertain Times* (Hanaway, 2019) was to consider the theoretical concept of what we might understand by the term 'existential leader', and then to go on to look at how an existential leader may approach some key leadership challenges. During the process of writing the book, it became clear that I had more to say on the theoretical level than I had anticipated, so my publishers and I decided to divide the original proposal into two separate books.

Of course, in business, as in life, the theoretical and practical are intimately entwined. I am not primarily a theoretician; my interest lies in how one applies theoretical and philosophical concepts in a simple practical way, particularly in areas of life where we may least except them, such as, in the business world. Our leadership roles are not confined to our professional life, and I believe the approach is just as useful in our personal life. However, in order to give this book a focus, I am looking at the ideas in the context of business and organisational leadership.

For this book to make sense to those of you who are new to the concept of existential leadership, I do need to outline my understanding of the term, and so the first chapter looks at the concept of leadership, and also at the main foci of existential thought.

I move on to consider how the two definitions of leadership and existentialism come together to create the idea of an existentially informed leader, who approaches the leadership task in relation to existential concepts.

From there, this book picks up where the first book left off. Although the word 'philosophy' is perhaps not the first that springs to mind when thinking about leadership, the importance of taking a philosophical approach in considering leadership is not new. Many people consider philosophy to be academic navel gazing, abstract and often unintelligible, and yet philosophy can be a real concrete tool in appropriate contexts, including the world of business and leadership. Philosophical thinking equips us to work with change through questioning the status quo. This ability is essential to any business.

Kotter (1999, p. 32) warned the business world that too many managers were being trained in and for *'a more stable world…that for the most part no longer exists'*, and Lowe (1998), in conversation with Jack Welch, CEO of GE, alerts us to the need for leaders to move from a primarily controlling and static mode to one based on guiding, energising and exciting. The old traditional assumptions based on scientific traditions are no longer relevant for today's world where change is rapid and the need for constant self-renewal, through critical self-questioning, is vital. Philosophical questioning is not about being clever, but as Socrates showed, it is about constantly questioning everything in order to challenge current perceptions and thus open up new ways of seeing and new possibilities. It is interesting to note that when Welch (2001, 2003) speaks of his leadership journey, he does not draw on management handbooks, but sees his learning and success as flowing from 'a philosophy' that came out of his journey. He was driven by the uncertainty of his time and situation. Uncertainty is a key truth in existential thought and something that I shall return to throughout this book. Blits (1989) draws particular attention to Socratic and Existential philosophy as frameworks through which we can use our own experiences to question abstractions and beliefs without translating them into certainty. This approach, often termed 'existential hermeneutic phenomenology', flows from the work of Martin Heidegger. Don't be put off by long, hard-to-pronounce words, and the often dense literature, in which the ideas are expressed. I aim to show how such thinking can help leaders with the very practical dilemmas they will encounter.

My own thinking on leadership owes much to my study and practice as an existential phenomenological psychotherapist. Another mouthful! When my younger daughter was very small she would practice saying it, rather like others might practice Mary Poppins's 'supercalifragilisticexpialidocious'. She declared that it had a similar magical effect in that when teachers or other authority figures asked what her mother did and she answered, 'She is an existential phenomenological psychotherapist', the conversation would stop there, and she was saved from further interrogation, with most adults wondering whether she was just making it up. In fact, it offers a very concrete approach to explore how each of us lives life and expresses our uniqueness in the world; the way we are 'being-in-the-world'.

These philosophical concepts, which at first glance may seem far removed from the world of work, have been drawn on by a number of leadership theorists. For example, Segal (2004, p. 27), when considering business approaches, looked to the philosophical counselling approach to provide responsive connection with the everyday realities of life, including professional life, knowing not just about *'one's psyche or personality but about the paradigms and worldviews that shape our professional practices'*. He considers that the discipline offers a clear and systematic way of looking at the role of leadership.

I call for a philosophical approach to leadership and as the philosophy, which personally speaks to me, is in the existential/phenomenological tradition, this provides the framework for my writing. I focus on how an existential leader may consider some of the inevitable practical and very real leadership challenges, drawing on the priorities implicit in an existential approach. The approach requires leaders to engage with a number of questions: Would the focus be different for a leader who was not existentially informed from one who is? If so, in what way and how might that affect them personally, and the whole philosophy and behaviour of their organisation? Is being an existential leader a positive in the business world? Is it sensible and practical to look to philosophy to guide a process which is often considered transactional rather than thoughtful? What does an existential leader look like?

These are all important questions and, in good existential fashion, I can say that I guarantee that I shall not be providing you with any definitive answers. Existentialism does not provide certainty but encourages us to embrace uncertainty and find our own meaning. In many ways, the answers are less important than the questions, as any answer will be contextual, individual and relational, and so based on personal perceptions and experience. Even two people attending the same MBA course and reading the same textbooks will have their own spin on what they read and hear, and their interpretation of their learning will change as they have their own experiences in business, or at least I would hope they do. I would suggest that for a leader to regularly ask themselves the kinds of existential questions posed in this book makes that person a different kind of leader, open to challenge and change, and so better placed to meet the leadership challenges of this uncertain century.

There are so many dilemmas and challenges which all leaders face that it was difficult to know where to start. I understand that I cannot address them all and hope that I have not left out something important to you as a leader. I trust that the book will provide leaders with a way of thinking existentially which is transferable to all leadership challenges. However, in order to structure my thinking in some way, I decided to group the challenges into three main areas,

Vision
Recruitment, retention and development of staff
Preventing, managing and resolving conflict

I believe that the broader questions of how to manage and develop the business flow from the concepts and ideas covered by these headings.

To have a business, one must first have an idea. Ideally, every business or organisation starts with a vision – preferably one which is clear, exciting and inspiring. The vision is usually led by the founder's values, beliefs, passions and dreams. So the formation of a company or organisation's vision seemed an appropriate place to start. In Chapter 2, I examine what constitutes a vision and how a vision can be existentially informed. It may sound strange – indeed, it does even to me – but I had great fun looking through the vision statements of a number of different-sized companies and discovering that unconsciously many did address existential issues, although never using that word. I offer some guidelines on how a vision can be created with existential concerns at its core.

Once the vision is established, then people are needed to implement that vision, or ideally even earlier, to co-create it. An organisation's people are its main and most important resource. How a leader recruits, retains and develops those people then becomes of paramount importance. There is no point having a vision which remains a paper exercise, no matter how inspiring it was to create. The leadership tasks of finding the 'right' people to embrace and implement the vision, and supporting them in that endeavour, are the focus of the next section in the book. I explore these three staff-related elements from an existential perspective. Included in this chapter is an introduction to existential coaching as one way of developing staff.

All leaders will encounter conflict, and so the next section focuses on preventing, managing and dealing with conflict. Conflicts can be small or grand in scale. Some conflicts can easily be resolved, and others may never be resolved, but still need to be managed. A leader needs to understand conflict and recognise that it is not always negative and can be used creatively. Leaders may experience conflict as an attack, experiencing it as disrespectful, a challenge to authority, an attempt to 'dethrone' them or an attack to the ego, or, alternatively, it can provide an opportunity for a leader to rethink and draw on the creativity of others in symbiosis with their own original ideas. I seek to explore these different reactions and consider the use of existentially informed conflict coaching and mediation as approaches for resolving conflict.

The challenges and dilemmas which leaders face are many and various. As stated, I am not attempting to list and address them all here, but I believe that the philosophical approach I have used to consider the areas I have focused on is transferable to all leadership challenges.

Part I

What do we mean by 'existential leadership'?

The very phrase 'existential leadership' immediately poses three questions which I shall seek to address as briefly as possible. Firstly, what do we understand by 'existential'; secondly, what does the word 'leadership' mean; and finally, how do the two come together to form a meaningful description of a particular leadership style, or, as I would prefer to think of it, 'way of being' as a leader?

In my previous book on the existential leader, I considered in some detail what I mean by 'existential leadership', starting with a brief history of existential thought and its practical usage. I do not propose to repeat that here. However, for the rest of what follows to make sense, it is important that I give a précis of my understanding of what existential leadership entails. Although covering some old ground, the chapter does reflect new reading and thinking. I move on from laying the foundations of what we understand by 'existential' and what we understand by 'leadership' and how together they form the existential leadership model to a further consideration of how some of these ideas can be put to practical use.

Chapter 1

What does it mean to be 'existential'?

The word 'existential' is becoming commonly used in the media to describe all manner of things. It can be considered a philosophical trend, tendency or attitude, as distinct from a particular dogma or system. However the media choose to understand and portray it, we should perhaps accept that even existential scholars are not in full agreement as to what constitutes existentialism. Whilst the deliberations of existentialist philosophers do not necessarily sit neatly with each other at all times, writers from the nineteenth and twentieth centuries such as Kierkegaard, Nietzsche, Heidegger, Jaspers, Marcel, de Beauvoir, Merleau-Ponty, Camus and Sartre would be in agreement with the singular notion that 'being' (with all its embodied, relational and emotional presence) has to take precedence over (rationalist) 'knowledge'.

Rationality appears to offer certainty, yet existentialists believe that we cannot hold much certainty about anything, even what we mean by 'existential'. Davis and Miller (1967, p. 206) noted that *'Man is an existential being whose life is more than logic and who must discover the meaning of existence. There are no answers to the human predicament to be found in the back of a book; Philosophy is to be lived, something to be proven in action.'* The answers to what makes an existential leader can also not be found on the back or even within a book. One has to truly discover the meaning by 'being' an existential leader.

Existentialists and phenomenologists believe that our human 'essence' is simply our 'existence' (being in the world). Existentialism is often connected with what are thought to be *negative* emotions, such as anxiety (worrying), dread (a very strong fear) and mortality (awareness of our own death). As a group willing to express these aspects of being, existentialists are deeply interested in emotions. Phenomenologists focus more on the nature and meaning of emotions and bring the study of emotions to the forefront of philosophical inquiry. Their interest lies in the ability of emotions to engage with reality. Emotions are always about some thing. An emotion is a way, perhaps the principal way, in which the world manifests itself to us. The theories of Sartre and Heidegger flow from a view of emotions as explored by Brentano, Husserl and Scheler, and further developed by Merleau-Ponty, Levinas and Ricoeur, with Robert Solomon, amongst others, bringing phenomenological theories to current agendas.

Emotions are intentional; they tell us something about ourselves and others, and are often felt in relation to the **values and beliefs** we hold. We get upset or happy about something because we value it, we believe in it, and it holds meaning for us. Existential thinking places considerable importance on our beliefs and our attempts to be true to them.

To be true, we must be aware, and existentialists place much value on the idea of the 'aware self', a thinking and feeling being with emotions, beliefs, hopes, fears, desires and the need to find meaning and purpose. It is not rationalist or empiricist in its philosophy, as the most important questions are not considered accessible to reason and science.

In this way, the approach differs from many approaches to leadership. As the ideas do not flow from rational disciplines, we must live our lives based on our own unique perception of the world, others in it and our understanding of our lived experiences. This draws on the work of Husserl (1859–1938), who described us as living in 'an interpreted world' in which we come to our own conclusions about the meaning we choose to give things. If everything is subjective, then it is easy for more scientific and rationalist theorists to dismiss existentialism. Heidegger, from whom many existential ideas flow, has been criticised for having an ontology that was not deductive or systematic in form and *'proceeds at times by the exegesis of poetry or the more aphoristic fragments of the pre-Socratic philosophers'* (McIntyre, 1967, p. 543). This led Sanderson (2004, p. 4) to declare that *'existential and phenomenological philosophers tend to "write from the soul" and their style is very subjective.'* These 'criticisms' notwithstanding, the existential approach offers a way of understanding the role of humans as agents in a fluid social setting. It is particularly suited to the uncertainty we are currently encountering, and Sanderson suggests that engagement with existential writers has never been more relevant. Existentialism and phenomenology do not give us 'truths' to fall back on. The approach requires us to 'bracket' all our assumptions and to focus on things as they appear in our experience: we are responsible for the way we experience things and the meaning we give to things as they arise and are experienced in our 'life-world'.

Despite not being systemic, existentialism is concerned with core concepts. Fundamentally, these are set within the acceptance that we experience our 'being' within the context of our **temporality**. We will not go on forever. One existential challenge is the willingness to embrace that our time on earth is limited – we shall all die. This makes the time between birth and death very precious. We cannot constantly hold the awareness of death. Yet, we encounter many endings along the way, not just the end of our physical embodiment, but also the death of hope, future, confidence, and the ending of relationships, jobs or courses. For the existentialist, it is vital to work to create a healthy balance between an awareness of death/loss and the propensity to become overwhelmed and terrified by it. Death is one of the greatest, if not the greatest, experiences of uncertainty; in death we face the ultimate 'not knowing'.

Tillich (1952) writes of the tremendous courage required to live life in the face of anxiety and death. In order to experience the true beauty of life, one has to become vulnerable to death and anxiety. To live with acceptance of death and uncertainty is to live **authentically**. We need to be aware of our motives, feelings, desires and self-relevant cognitions, and not deny, distort or ignore internal experiences and external information. We must act in tune with our true self, beliefs and values. Living authentically is not easy. For Sartre, the 'vertiginous' experience of the recognition of our freedom and choices can feel so unbearable that some people choose to live inauthentically or, as Sartre would describe it, live 'in bad faith' rather than engage with life.

Being constantly and fully authentic is an idealised aim. Erickson (1995) and Heidegger (1962) speak of the 'level' of authenticity in a person, as people are never entirely authentic or inauthentic but seek to achieve a *level* of authenticity. Remaining authentic can be a lonely experience, as we tend to fall under the sway of others. To be 'different' can be hard, and it can prove tempting to slip into banality and fail to think. Existentialism requires us to acknowledge our anxiety, and its causes, and to live **authentically** with the knowledge that there is no meaning other than the meaning we find for ourselves. This is an invitation to creativity, for those who wish to hear it. To live as though things are certain, or to ignore our values and beliefs, would be an example of living in **bad faith**; we must create our own meaning.

We each live our own unique lives as autonomous beings with freedom and responsibility, but there are a number of things we all share – death, freedom, responsibility, existential isolation and meaninglessness (Yalom, 1980). We can also add relatedness, uncertainty, emotionality and anxiety to that list.

We do not live our lives alone, but in relation to others and the things around us. In this existential aspect of **relatedness** we experience ourselves, and everything around us, the world, other people, us included, in the context of a relationship. Within these relationships we encounter **uncertainty**. Life is uncertain in its meaning and our futures are uncertain. This uncertainty causes an existential **anxiety** that is all pervading and endless.

Much of human existence can become a battle to deny our anxiety about the uncertainty and meaninglessness of life. One way of trying to defeat these enemies is to seek power in the mistaken belief that it can offer certainty and an escape from powerlessness and **temporality**. Throughout his writings, Camus sees the hopeless human desire to make sense of our condition and to establish certainty where it does not exist as being essentially absurd and impossible. He challenges us to respond appropriately to this situation and to live in full consciousness of our state of uncertainty and absurdity. If we can accept these absurdities, we can liberate ourselves from habit and convention, bringing about a 'passion' to live intensely, not to escape the sense of absurdity, but to face it with absolute lucidity. Kierkegaard challenges us in the absence of certainty and the need for passion to find a truth that is true for each of us individually and by which we can live or die. Anxiety is not considered a bad thing. Kierkegaard (1844, p. 155, 1980) wrote, '*Whoever has learned to be anxious in the right way has learned the ultimate*'.

If nothing is set in stone, then we have **freedom** in how we live our lives. As relational beings, this freedom carries responsibility. However, this existential freedom is not an espousal of a doctrine of total freedom. We are not free to decide to be born into this world or time. Existentialists term this 'throwness'. We are thrown into an existence we did not choose. However, once here, we are free to choose what we make of our lives. This is far from an easy task, which we often try hard to avoid in a number of ways. Currently we are all encouraged to use our freedom to think positively, something which Cerulo (2006) calls 'optimistic bias': an element of self-delusion, leaving us ill prepared to face uncertainty at those moments when it is most present for us. O'Gorman (2016, p. xiii) suggests that we can also choose to do the opposite, '...*worrying is also an attempt to control the unknown. Worrying is, among other things, a "futures management technique"... an attempt to assert some authority over what is ahead'.*

If we are to find meaning, it is through our **beliefs**. If we believe in something, it gives us meaning and lessens our anxiety, making some sense of the world for us. However, beliefs can become 'sedimented' or stuck. We can fail to question whether we still believe something and continue to live as though we do. This may be comforting, but it does not serve us well. It can take hard work to loosen these sedimented beliefs when they appear to offer us ways of defining the self-construct, creating a feeling of stability and security and acting as a guard against uncertainty.

During the twentieth century, existential and phenomenological ideas were brought into the practise of psychotherapy in Europe through the works of van Deurzen and Spinelli, amongst others. In their very accessible books they provide an understanding of the development of existential phenomenology and how the elements described in this book are used to explore the worldviews of clients.

Our understanding of the existential is not static. Recently Caruso and Flanagan (2018) have looked at how the growth in neuroscience fits alongside existentialism. They suggest that new neurobiological research confirms the existentialist view that we have no fixed soul or self and no inherent purpose. They believe that we exist as tiny specks on a small planet, within a wider universe, a concept referred to as 'naturalism'. This concept stresses the 'smallness' of each individual and can leave many people feeling deeply uneasy, experiencing ontological anxiety or angst, leading them to embark on a search for meaning. Caruso and Flanagan (2018, preface) term this recognition of individual insignificance a crisis of 'neuroexistentialism', suggesting that, '*Today there is a third-wave existentialism, neuroexistentialism which expresses the anxiety that, even as science yields the truth about human nature, it also disenchants.*' For those of us not intent on seeking certainty, we do not look to science to reveal undeniable truths. How often have scientific findings been turned on their head as new information and understanding come to light? Yet for many people science continues to hold out the hope of finding the 'right' and 'final' answers, which would bring certainty on some matters. We certainly need the benefits which scientific discovery brings; it can improve our daily material existence, but it cannot answer our existential questions. It is possible to live without a sense of certainty and to experience its lack positively, as a blank canvas on which to create.

In their thinking, Caruso and Flanagan define existentialism as the diminishment of the self-image caused by deep social or political changes. This immediately takes it beyond the philosophical and academic into daily life and into the world of work. They suggest that contemporary existential angst arises from the growing body of knowledge that shows the existence we experience to be a result of neural processes. Given this belief, their findings suggest that introspection or self-knowledge can't really reveal the mind, and that death is the end for us all. I do not think that existential reflection is intent on revealing the 'mind' or in some way 'defeating death', but more about providing an opening to the better understanding of our individual temporal human existence, an embodied experience which I would not solely locate in the mind. If the brain's processes give us our experience of life and there is no spirit or soul, then when the brain stops functioning, nothing follows life, and nothing survives us. Caruso and Flanagan contest Nietzsche's übermensch (the person who could rise above conventional Christian morality to create and impose his own values and thus overcome the loss of god) introduced in *Thus Spake Zarathustra* (1883–5). To their minds, this understanding of ourselves as animals governed by natural laws and physical mechanisms heralds another loss: the sense of agency or free will. I see this as a challenge to the centrality of the concept of existential free will and although I concur with most of what they suggest, on this point we differ. Knowing more about neuroscience does not mean we can abdicate our responsibility to make choices and take responsibility for the outcomes.

The belief that the human brain evolved to seek meaning, a task which is made increasingly hard, in Caruso and Flanagan's view, through the loss of religion, *'the sense of meaningfulness provided by religion is not so easily replicated in nonreligious settings'* (p. 287), coupled with the findings of cosmologists, such as Sean Carroll, from the California Institute of Technology, who concluded that there was no essential meaning in the universe, still lead to the belief that life matters on a personal and human scale, even when *'modern science has thoroughly undermined any hopes for a higher purpose or meaning inherent in the universe itself'* (ibid.). Carroll believes that our lives matter simply because we exist and coexist, and appreciate meaning, and not because we are part of some grand cosmic plan.

Michael Gazzinga (2012), from the University of California's SAGE Center for the Study of the Mind, also concludes that we are responsible and moral because our brains have evolved capabilities that allow us to be, and so although living in a universe which is random, within human experience we have certain obligations and capacities which we cannot ignore, whilst Thomas Clark (2016) of Brandeis University speaks of humans as being intuitively hard wired about ethics. So, once again the challenge is thrown to each of us to find our own personal meaning and identity and navigate our own moral and ethical path through life.

The above is merely an overview of some important aspects of existential thinking in order to set what is to follow, regarding leadership, into that existential context. In summary, existentialism is about the human condition and calls on each of us to live truthfully and authentically, from a starting point of life having no meaning other than the one we choose to give it. Inner conflict and anxiety result from the individual's confrontation with the givens of existence – the inevitability of death, freedom and its attendant responsibility, existential isolation and meaninglessness. Overall, existentialism is concerned with the meaning and problem of existence. This extends beyond our inner psychological life and our external social and public life into our working life, whilst at the same time holding in mind our spiritual life. Existential thinkers have developed a framework to explore how these existential issues are present in different aspects or 'dimensions' of our lives. I shall be referring to these throughout the book.

The four existential dimensions

Whilst remaining a grounded, authentic and secure individual, we all know that we do not always feel the same, or act the same, in all contexts. We choose to share different aspects of ourselves with different people at different times. We may feel confident about singing and dancing at a party, yet would not choose to do so in the workplace. We choose with whom to share our most intimate thoughts and desires, whereas there are others with whom we only react on a predominantly transactional or superficial level.

We exist slightly differently in the different contexts in which we operate. These contexts can be grouped into four dimensions of human existence – the physical (known as the Umwelt), the social (Mitwelt), the personal (Eigenwelt) and the spiritual (Überwelt). Readers coming from a business leadership background may see the connection between these dimensions and Deal's (2003) four frames of organisational behaviour: structural, human resource, political and culture. We can find the core aspects of relatedness, uncertainty and authenticity introduced above, in all dimensions, although they may be more developed in some than others.

Figure 1.1 shows the four core dimensions in which we exist. The arrows in the diagram seek to remind us that the degree to which each dimension is prominent will vary over time.

The physical dimension (Umwelt) is concerned with our response to the environment and the natural world, our body, surroundings, landscape, climate, objects and material possessions. The focus of the social dimension (Mitwelt) is on the way we relate to others in the public world around us, our response to the culture in which we live and the class and race we consider ourselves to belong to. The psychological dimension (Eigenwelt) focuses on the way individuals relate to themselves and create a personal world. This includes views about their own character, past experience and future possibilities. People search for a sense of identity, a feeling of being substantial and having a self. Inevitably many events will confront them with evidence to the contrary and plunge them into a state of confusion or disintegration. Finally, the spiritual dimension (Überwelt) relates to the ways in which individuals create a sense of an ideal world, an ideology and a

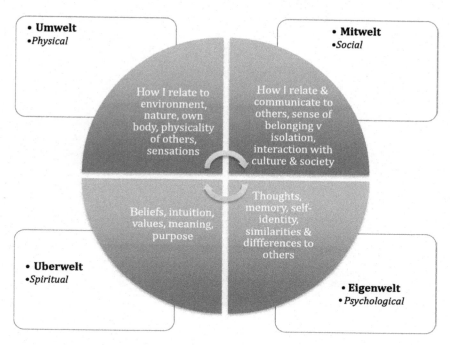

Figure 1.1 Hanaway (2013) existential dimensions.

philosophical outlook. It is here we find meaning by putting all the pieces of the puzzle together. People create their values through a search for something that matters enough 'to live or die for', something that may even hold ultimate and universal validity.

Through reflection on these existential dimensions and the acceptance and consideration of the existential givens, a leader can develop a good understanding of the sense of 'being' carried by themselves and each individual they work with. They gain an understanding of how they are in the world and how they relate to it in all its complexity.

Chapter 2

What does it mean to be a leader?

We find leaders in most societies and cultures. There are very few examples of truly leaderless communities, groups or businesses, although there is a strategy of '*leaderless resistance, or phantom cell structure*', a social resistance strategy in which small, independent groups including individuals challenge an established institution such as a law, economic system, social order, government and so on. While it lacks a central command, the concept includes a common goal between the individual and the group or social movement from which the ideology grew. Even if there appears to be no named or material leader, if we look closely there is usually a symbolic figurehead who sets objectives and identifies targets. This may not be a living, breathing person but could be a written or verbal doctrine.

It would seem we like the idea of leadership. Indeed, it may not merely be that we **like** the idea, but we may believe that we **need** leaders. If we look to the animal kingdom, we also see examples of leadership. Packs of animals have leaders. Often it is a position which is fought over until one animal retreats in ignominious defeat, or indeed loses its life. As an owner of two female dogs of the same breed, I can also see how leadership is played out there. Even though the younger one is bigger and stronger, on most things she defers to the older dog.

I suggest that in humans, this 'need' for a leader stems from deep existential needs to address or guard against our existential concerns, including our paradoxical relationship with freedom, our understanding of relatedness and our desire for certainty and meaning. We may look to leaders to help us with these fundamental existential dilemmas. The meaning we seek by accepting a leader and being a follower may not be anything deeply philosophical. In the work context, it may simply be meaningful because it provides us with payment. What we do with that payment may hold deeper meaning – we can use it to secure our survival. The survival itself is the most meaningful aspect, but the processes involved in securing it take on a meaning through having that as the goal.

At the core of our human condition lies the immutable reality that we can neither predict nor totally control our destiny (existential uncertainty), and this knowledge challenges our sense of mastery and efficiency, leading to deep-seated dread (existential anxiety). To follow a leader provides us with a project through which we can find meaning. A leader is future oriented, and as such can help us to believe in the 'illusional certainty' of the future. The leader seduces us with five-year plans and long-term strategies, helping us to ignore time, temporality and ultimately 'death' (as represented by retirement, redundancy, redeployment or dismissal).

Leaders also allow us the opportunity to disengage from the responsibility of our freedom. Instead of owning our choices and decisions, we can pass this responsibility onto someone else – our leader. Thus the existence of a leader can seemingly act as a guard against uncertainty and ontological anxiety whilst enabling us to ward off responsibility. This feeling of security does not come without cost. In return we choose to be subservient and obedient.

There are costs to the designated leader, too. It is often 'lonely at the top', and leaders suffer their own existential fears. If leaders lose their followers, they are no longer leaders. A leader may interpret their leadership position as evidence that they are in control of their destiny. This is never truly the case.

If we accept that we choose to appoint leaders, or at least accept their right to leadership, this raises the question of what it is that makes them different and causes us to treat them as special. It may be concerned with their personality and charisma or the skills and knowledge they have acquired. Or it may be more about our need to be led, guided, nurtured and supported throughout our lives at all levels and in all situations.

Theorists have struggled to come up with a universal definition of what constitutes a leader, or what distinguishes *effective* leaders from *ineffective* leaders (Bennis and Nanus, 1997). The requirements of a leader are contextual and situational; a style of leadership which works well in one situation may not succeed in another. I have previously considered the different styles and traits of leaders (Hanaway, 2019), and in this context it is sufficient to note that they range through varied continuums between the autocratic and the democratic, the task oriented and the relationship oriented, the bureaucratic and the laissez-faire. Simplistically, one could say that leadership styles span a spectrum from autocratic to participative (Likert, 1967). Amongst the leadership styles identified and written about are the transactional, which focuses on directing people how to undertake a task and rewarding them for obedience, and the transformational, which is more concerned with engaging, supporting and developing staff. The transactional approach requires a 'blind' commitment of the follower, based on a belief that by acquiring the title 'leader', the obedience of the follower is implicit. This type of leadership may be essential in some contexts, for example, on the battlefield where a quick response to a leadership command may be the difference between life and death. For this reason, the most common style of postwar leadership was transactional, with many business leaders having served as military leaders. The 1960s brought in social, moral and economic changes and a more transformative leadership approach. Transformational leaders need to be inspirational and to develop a vision in which they believe and which is congruent with their personal and professional values and beliefs. It is therefore more closely aligned with the existential need for meaning based on values than a transactional approach would be. Overall, transformational leaders are considered to use high levels of emotional intelligence, be charismatic and show exemplary standards of consistency and integrity.

There are many subsets of these leadership styles. These include the **charismatic leader**, of which there are both transactional and transformative examples. This style is deemed to stem from the leader's 'mana' or divine right to leadership. Charismatic leaders often appear at times of great distress when a radical vision is needed to resolve a crisis. We can also identify their antithesis in the **quiet leader**, who bases their success not on ego and force of character, but on their thoughts and actions. They believe that their actions speak louder than their words and that through giving people credit for their work they are more motivated than when the leader takes credit.

Some leadership models place greater emphasis than others on the growth and well-being of the people and communities they are associated with. **Servant leaders** provide an example of this. They aim to share power, prioritise the needs of others before their own and support people to maximise their development and performance.

We all have a particular style of leadership which we prefer or are more inclined to use when we lead. In the 1960s McGregor proposed a theory, termed the X and Y theory, in which he explored these different preferences, concluding that every leader could be categorised as either an 'X' or a 'Y' (McGregor, 2006). X leaders consider that humans have an inherent dislike for work and will avoid it wherever possible, preferring the security of being directed and avoiding responsibility. An 'X' leader will attempt to counter this dislike by controlling, directing, coercing, threatening and punishing employees in order to get them to work. In contrast, Y leaders propose that humans have a natural desire to work and pursue challenging goals, and expect to find work a source of satisfaction, fulfilment and enjoyment. This leads a Y leader to trust and engage people, allowing them to work productively and effectively in a self-controlled and self-directed manner. Blake and Mouton (1964) developed a Managerial Grid which also identifies five different leadership styles based on a grid, plotting the extent to which a leader was focused on task or people.

Followers, too, will have styles which work better for them. Some people value clear detailed instructions, whereas others find these frustrating and need to have some opportunity to bring in their own creativity. They will be at their happiest and most productive when the leadership style matches their preference.

Chapter 3

The challenge of finding a new type of leadership for the 21st century

What is considered good leadership changes over time to fit current needs. Today, economic and political uncertainty, the digital explosion, dramatic changes in customer and employee behaviour and the increased pace of change mean it is increasingly difficult to drive growth and create competitive advantage. These factors present leaders with crucial new challenges. In addition, the nature and pattern of work have always changed and evolved. Each decade presents new challenges and opportunities. We have moved from the industrial age to the information age. A company's intangible assets such as intellectual property, winning brands, innovative ideas and, most importantly, talented staff are now equally, if not more, important than its hard assets. We see an increase in people's skills being transferable and individuals' expectations of the developmental, financial and psychological rewards increasing, together with higher behavioural standards for the workplace.

We are faced with new challenges in the workplace. We have an overload of information, much of it digital. The working lifespan has grown, with many people working well beyond pension age. The young worker, more used to the digital world, and the person approaching retirement will each be looking to their work to provide relevant meaning for the phase of life they are currently in.

This diverse workforce requires leaders to be aware of and sensitive to the worldviews of all the people they are working with. Sensitivity to the uniqueness of individual worldviews is central to an existential approach. We gain access to others' worldviews, hopes, fears, values and beliefs through genuine interest and through listening. People are less likely than in previous generations to accept a nonactive role in the development of the company they work for. They will have an expectation (in some cases a legal right) to be consulted on decisions leading to changes in their conditions of service. An existential leader will welcome dialogue and wish to be creative, honest and open in their leadership approach. They understand the importance of others (relatedness) with their different perceptions of the world. For an existential leader, there needs to be an authentic commitment to listen and, where appropriate, to take heed of what is being said and bring about change in line with the recommendations coming from any participative consultations.

Whilst seeing an increase in participation, we are also experiencing an increase in rules and regulations. This may appear a paradox with the promise of greater openness in communication being partnered with a narrowing of acceptable behaviours and a decrease in freedom. Although many regulations are questionable and potentially restrictive, the majority have been introduced to address specific needs, particularly in the field of health and safety. Inevitably with more regulations comes more bureaucracy, with many processes appearing meaningless.

If we can succeed in finding our way through the red tape, we still have the problem of finding and keeping excellent staff. In a number of recent reports, Kinsey Management Consultants have warned us that talented staff are increasingly sought after, and businesses are in competition to attract them, requiring employers to think creatively as to how to both attract and retain talented people. Employees' needs are becoming more diverse and complex, and it is increasingly necessary to offer different ways of working such as home working, virtual working and part-time working and to face the challenges of accommodating maternity, paternity and carer leave together with the desire for career breaks.

These new ways of working are set within the increase in globalisation which has proved a catalyst for many of the changes, with Rothkop (1997, p. 1) suggesting that on an existential level, this is *'the first time in history that virtually every individual at every level of society can sense the impact of international changes. They can see and hear it in their media, taste it in their food, and sense it in the products that they buy'*. The idea of the 'global' is evidenced in all areas of our lives such as politics, business, industry, crime, culture, language, education, community, terrorism, communications, music, cuisine, company and environment. We even hear talk of the global person: the 'global me', a hybridised, cultural 'mongrel' and a true citizen of the world (Zachary, 2000). Depending upon your point of view, globalisation is the phenomenon that will either make or break humanity's ability to survive beyond the next few hundred years. Goldmark (2002, p. 59) states succinctly, *'the future is open and little is certain. The stakes are enormous'*, whilst Held, McGrew, Goldblatt and Perraton (1999, p. 16) describe the essence of current globalisation as *'a transformation in the spatial organisation of social relations and transactions – assessed in terms of their extensity, intensity, velocity and impact – generating transcontinental or interregional flows and networks of activity, interaction, and the exercise of power'*. This opening of frontiers can feel stimulating, exciting and an invitation to innovation. Yet, we know that most people crave certainty, so this opening up to the unknown can also cause increased anxiety. Giddens (1999, p. 1) describes this as being in a *'runaway world'*, creating a kind of Sartrean nausea, with little-understood global processes affecting almost every aspect of what we do, not always for the better. Others, like Singer (2002, p. 11) are concerned that globalisation is *'out of control'*, and Sanderson (2004, p. 6) contrasts the developed world entering into the twentieth century with *'huge expectations and excitement, the same ebullience'* with the challenges of the twenty-first century, when we must, *'Enter the existential component to our lives in the sense that it is timely to talk about the problem of simply "being" in a universe that seems to be less determined, less ordered and less controllable than what rationalists and empiricists would have had us believe in the past few hundred years'* (ibid.).

Hand in hand with these feelings of lack of control and the need for existential reflection, globalisation brings greater awareness of how others exist. This brings fresh expectations of fairness and interpretations of trust and justice. It is now much easier to cross-compare how we are treated and to see differences in pricing, taxation and other processes.

This increased global knowledge and the potential to build global alliances has seen an increase of global activism, particularly in the areas of global poverty and environmentalism. There are increasing demands for organisations to focus not just on financial success, but to take a greater responsibility for the impact of their work on people (mitwelt) and the environment (umwelt). This requires a more ethical approach. Issues such as modern slavery are being taken seriously. Some industries are responding to the new challenges created by increased diversity of diet, especially through the growing interest in veganism and vegetarianism, increased interest in more ecological transport and the demand for more consideration to be given to the environmental impact of their products both in their use and in their final disposal. These developments are evidence that we cannot rely on certainty, as the world is constantly changing. The future is not easy to predict. Leaders must acknowledge and work with that uncertainty by being creative and collaborative, both key elements in an existential approach. Work needs to be meaningful, and what is meaningful one day may not be so the next. We are faced with using our existential freedom ethically and taking full responsibility for our decisions.

We can see evidence of the existential anxiety that many of these new challenges are producing. Suicide, depression and anxiety are on the rise. The behavioural scientist Clay Rutledge does not put this down merely to the lack of adequate mental health service but sees it as the result of a *'crisis of meaningless'*. Writing in the *Dallas News* in 2018, he explained that, *'in order to keep existential anxiety at bay, we must find and maintain perceptions of our lives as meaningful. We are a species which strives not just for survival, but also for significance'*. The lack of meaning makes people psychologically vulnerable.

Caruso and Flanagan (2018) see the twenty-first century also as a time of philosophical crisis, a time which is neither ecclesiastical or political, but which has its roots in the new scientific discoveries, resulting in a clash between the scientific and humanistic ways in which we see people. They call for us to *'make use of the knowledge and insights of behavioural, cognitive, and neurosciences to satisfy our existential concerns and achieve some level of flourishing and fulfillment'* (p. 11).

Facing these challenges requires bold leaders, *'bold enough to lead in this age of uncertainty'* by employing *'a new kind of leadership'* (Boyatizis and McKee, 2005, p. 1). Leadership theorists have moved away from focusing on transactional aspects of leadership and begun to focus their attention on the growing need for work to offer more than the exchange of service for payment. Quite hard-nosed

CEOs like Jack Welch of GE see the need to change from scientific management, which was intent on control, to an approach aimed at guiding, energising and exciting those who follow him (Lowe, 1998). This represents a move from the reliance on management handbooks and management skills training to the development of a philosophy in the face of uncertainty where old conventions were no longer relevant. Thus the challenges for leaders in the twenty-first century are not just behavioural, but psychological and philosophical.

These new challenges require different ways of managing people and processes which are more in line with the needs and culture of the twenty-first century. New ways of thinking about leadership are emerging. These leadership approaches include Connective Leadership, Authentic Leadership, Responsible Leadership, Resonant Leadership and Humble Leadership. All draw on the identified need for greater emotional intelligence in the leadership sphere and place a greater importance on the personal and relational. Although each approach has its own focus, I suggest that they all share an existential approach, whether this is conscious and acknowledged or not.

All these approaches draw on Daniel Goleman's (1995) work on Emotional Intelligence (EI or EQ) which references intelligence, neuroscience and psychology. I have given a little more information about EI in my previous book (Hanaway, 2019), but at the core is the belief that more than a rational approach is needed in relation to leadership. The model focuses on competencies and skills covering five areas: self-awareness, self-regulation, social skill, empathy and motivation. Emotionally intelligent leaders bring the existential elements of authenticity, the relational nature of presence and a mindful approach to their leadership roles and responsibilities.

Others have built on the emotional intelligence approach. At the start of the century, Lipman-Blumen (2000) produced 'Connective Leadership', calling for a more connected and meaningful approach to leadership in the light of increased globalisation. Connective leadership has at its heart a **relational** approach which it shares with the existential, focusing on various modes of working with and through other people, whilst noting and working sensitively with the shifts in geopolitics. The approach looks to find common meaning to inspire people despite diversity in order to commit to organisational values.

Writers such as Rickards and Clark (2006), drawing on the 1970s work of Smircich and Morgan, amongst others, take a broader and more philosophical look at the dilemmas of leadership. They place '**meaning**' at the heart of leadership, believing leadership to be **primarily** about 'the management of meaning'. They concern themselves with personal map-making, creative leadership, meaning and myths, rationality and freedom, ethics and equality. We can see how closely these are connected with key existential issues of relatedness, uncertainty, anxiety, meaning, freedom and authenticity. Indeed, in their consideration of a new leadership approach fit for the new century, they talk of a '*shift from a belief in scientific and observable reality, to a socially constructed reality, with the emphasis on meanings and symbolism*' (Rickards and Clark, 2006, p. 103).

This draws on the philosophy of Husserl, which is clearly described in Spinelli's 1989 book *The Interpreted World*. We all respond to the uncertainty and lack of ultimate, universal meaning in the world by seeking to create a sense of our existence through finding our own meaning through our own unique interpretation of the world. This is as true in our professional life as it is in our personal life.

The existential theme of **authenticity** has also been central in the thinking of other leadership theorists. Despite Solomon and Fernando's (2018, p. 149) claim that, *'authentic leaders do not know what they are doing'*, they go on to state, *'what they have is a vision, a direction, and a keen sense of confidence in themselves'*. They do not know what they are doing because they are authentically open to flexibility and change, and are willing to listen to their intuition and to other people. This demonstrates a trust in themselves and a passion for living by the truth as they see it. Authentic leaders are not only true to themselves, but also to their roles as leaders, whilst being aware of social cues and followers' needs, expectations, desires and feedback (Day and Kilduff, 2003; Kernis, 2003). To be true to oneself, one has to be self aware and to reflect on and challenge one's self-concept. Such critical self-reflection helps authentic leaders to know themselves and gain clarity and concordance in relation to their core values, beliefs, identity, emotions, goals and motives. This openness to self-criticism and commitment and to being honest inspires trust in those looking to them for leadership.

Not everyone embraces authentic leadership. Some theorists have been critical of the approach, with Pfeffer (2015) warning us that in his opinion, the last thing a leader needs to be at crucial moments is authentic. Ibarra is also critical, believing *'We have to find a way to fake it till we become it'*, (2015, p. 54) and Adam Grant also claims that to, *'"Be yourself" is actually terrible advice...Nobody wants to see your true self'* (2016, p. 4).

It is not easy to take an authentic approach, as it requires us to set aside preoccupations with 'to-do' lists in order to reflect and focus on the truth of relational aspects of leadership, including seeking honest feedback from colleagues, friends and subordinates.

Any authentic approach requires a leader to be mindful. This theme has been picked up by many recent writers, including Boyatzis and McKee (2005), who consider what it is to be a 'Resonant' leader. They place mindfulness, hope and compassion high on the list of requirements, calling for a mindful approach that involves living in a state of full conscious awareness of one's whole self, other people and our context. This again draws on the centrality of relatedness. Like the Servant leader, a Resonant leader uses a degree of self sacrifice and also needs to attend to their self care – developing their intellect, taking care of their bodies and attending to deeply held beliefs and values which feed the spirit. These echo the existential dimensions – social, physical, psychological and spiritual, setting leadership within a relational framework (in relation to self, others, nature and society).

More recently, Tim Richardson (2015) published *The Responsible Leader*. Although many of the concepts are similar to those of existential leadership, the philosophical background and emphasis do differ. Richardson focuses on the existential quest for **certainty**. He describes the world as VUCA – volatile, uncertain, complex and ambiguous – and calls for responsible leaders with a sense of self and clarity of identity, values and ethics. He stresses the importance of thinking and operating relationally, explaining that a responsible leader needs to be adaptable whilst remaining clear about their values so as to lead with the aid of 'a moral compass'. As with existential thinking, he sees the world as *'ambiguous'* and calls for leaders to be comfortable with *'not knowing'*. This requires them to be open and confident, whilst at the same time adopting a humble approach. Just as in the existential approach, he does not see leadership as a set of skills, but as a way of being, calling for responsible leaders to see the bigger picture and be **intentional** (**intentionality** being a major tenet of existential thought), to **choose** to be **morally accountable**, acting for the greater good (in line with the existential emphasis on **responsibility** and **freedom of choice**, based on a set of **values**) and to care about others, enabling them to be creative (this links to the importance of **relatedness** in the existential approach).

Richardson's requirement for humility is picked up in Schein and Schein's *Humble Leadership* (2018). They propose an essentially relational and cooperative approach, pointing out that leadership can rotate and also come from a group of people rather than just a designated leader. For them, '*...leadership is always a **relationship**'*, with successful leaders thriving on *'a group culture of high openness and high trust'* (p. ix). They position humble leadership not as a separate approach, but as the process or dynamic within other approaches, just as the existential may be seen as an underlying philosophy on which other structures can grow. The approach moves away from offering lists of required skills. They consider that leadership prescriptions founded on the beliefs that we need heroes and which praise individualism are outmoded. Instead, Schein and Schein believe that the desire to improve leadership skills flows from a more collective desire to help groups perform better. They see leadership as having four tiers. The first is designated as 'minus 1' and is based on *'total impersonal domination and coercion'*. Level 1 is where the focus is on *'transactional role and rule-based supervision, service, and most forms of "professional" helping relationships'*. Level 2 consists of *'personal cooperative, trusting relationships as in friendships and in effective teams'*. Finally there is level 3, in which they place humble leadership. At this level the focus is *'emotionally intimate'*, based on *'total mutual commitments'* (p. 27).

Chapter 4

What challenges does existentialism bring to leadership?

Having looked at a brief overview of the key elements of existential thought and some of the different styles and models of leadership, we can move on to what I understand by the term 'existential leadership' and how these existential elements are lived out by an existential leader.

Existential leaders build their leadership approach around the existential beliefs and concerns of uncertainty, authenticity, relatedness, freedom and meaning. In doing so they seek to bring together a philosophical and psychological approach in the context of a business environment, where pragmatic needs must also be addressed. The approach requires a deep awareness of and attention to the existential human givens – our need for self-esteem, the need to be heard, the importance of time and temporality, the core place of values and beliefs, the human requirement for meaning, our experience and dread of uncertainty and our emotional engagement with ourselves, others and the world.

Increasingly we are looking to the time we spend in work to address some of these existential concerns which revolve around our need to live, to love, to learn and to leave a legacy (Covey, 2004). Despite these perhaps sounding quite ethereal and idealistic, the existential leadership approach is very practical. I intend to focus on the main existential concerns separately as each contains a challenge to leaders.

The existential challenges of leadership

The challenge of relatedness

The emphasis on relatedness calls for leaders to value those they work with and pay attention to the importance of recruiting and retaining the best people. All of this is set in the context of an authentic and meaningful relationship.

The key to business development and success is understanding your main resource – your people. Once appointed, in order to fulfil their potential, people need to be supported and developed. They need to find the post meaningful, to feel seen, heard, valued and respected. In order to understand them as individuals, not just as the cogs which make your business wheels function, you need to understand their psychology, their worldview. A leader may choose to do this in a number of ways. They may involve professionals outside the organisation to offer consultancy, training, coaching and support. Internally they can give regular and authentic feedback based on a real understanding of the identified strengths and weaknesses of the individual, and the team. At its simplest, it means the leader getting to know the people they work with. I have devoted a later chapter to how existential leaders appoint, retain and develop staff.

The emphasis the existential approach places on relatedness means that the existential approach is also well positioned to work with issues of diversity, a necessity for today's leader in a global and multicultural world. This may be a surprising statement given the links which have been made with some existential writers and Nazism. I shall not analyse or defend these here, but instead focus on what the approach offers to us in relating to and with those from other cultures, races, religions, genders, sexual orientations, classes and backgrounds than our own.

Existential thinkers, including Sartre and Beauvoir, have explicitly considered the place of the 'Other' (that is, the person perceived to be unlike me) in our thinking and in our ways of being-in-the-world. Sartre agrees with Heidegger that the relation to the other is a relation of being, not an epistemological one. Beauvoir's concern with the self-other relation is clear from the beginning of her career. Her second fictional work, *The Blood of Others* (1945, epigraph) carries a quotation from Dostoevsky's *The Brothers Karamazov*. '*Each of us is responsible for everything and to every human being*', which neatly encapsulates the interflow of relatedness.

Anderson (2019) draws to our attention that, in writing about Otherness in her theory of alterity, Beauvoir distinguishes between two forms of otherness: existential alterity and sociopolitical. The sociopolitical results from oppression of both individuals and groups, while existential alterity is seen as a necessary feature of the human condition that discloses the foreignness of the other as a freedom. We can see this leading to an ethic of reciprocity.

Sartre is known for his stand against anti-Semitism and his participation, alongside Fanon, in the Algerian Front de Libération Nationale. He wrote prefaces for the works of powerful writers such as Fanon, Senghor and Memmi, who focused on race and otherness. Judaken (2008) claims that in his *Dialectical Reason*, Sartre anticipated and laid the foundations for much of the work undertaken in 'race' critical theories, evidencing this in a number ways.

Indeed, Sartre was one of the first to see 'race' as a social construct, insisting that '"race" is formed by social struggles and informs processes of inclusion and exclusion, racial subjectification and subjection'. From this belief he developed 'the dialectic of the gaze as intrinsic to defining the individual and collective Self and Other', criticizing 'the shortcomings of the liberal, humanist, Enlightenment tradition for combating racism'. He went on to examine 'how racism was shaped in discourse – considering the semiology of the racialised other and the necessity to deconstruct these stereotypes' and saw discrimination as 'institutionalized in *the structures and rituals of everyday life'* and how *'rules and norms establishing hierarchy and subjugation within the social order could be revealed from the perspective of the racially oppressed'*. Over time he came to appreciate *'how race and racism function within the neocolonial global order'* (Judaken, 2008, pp. 8–9). All of these are worth considering by leaders, reflecting on relatedness with those we work with in both global and national contexts.

Cultural competency has become one of the buzz phrases in the field of business and leadership. It has been defined as including multicultural awareness, knowledge and skill (Sue, Arredondo, & McDavis, 1992; Sue et al., 1982). Each person is not that dissimilar from another, and yet we are all unique. We all have the same two sets of chromosomes and genes. All are organised in (nearly) the same order. We make (almost) all the same chemistry to develop our bodies, digest our food, extract energy and circulate oxygen in and carbon dioxide out and are made up of trillions of the same types of cells. We all have blood moving oxygen and carbon dioxide in our arteries and veins. We all have the same immune system (though we have all been sensitised to different things). The observable differences are really quite trivial. Our embodied selves share the same challenges of physical survival, and we face the same philosophical and existential dilemmas. The degree and manner in which we engage with, understand and deal with them will differ, as will the context in which we experience them.

Diversity is an issue because it requires us to engage with the unknown, and in doing so we are faced with uncertainty. This can be a very knotty issue, for example, in an ongoing debate between some male-to-female transgender people and some feminists. Here is not the place to analyse the different perspectives, but the question being posed is a complex one concerning knowing and not knowing. There is much anger amongst some transgender women that some feminists do not see them as women. These feminists ask how a person can be known as a woman if they have not experienced certain things. How can one be considered a woman if one hasn't navigated the period of bodily change, outside their control, which girls experience at puberty? What is it to be a woman who has not experienced monthly bleeds, or become fearful at the nonappearance of those bleeds, or feels less of a woman if they never experience periods or their cessation at menopause? These and similar questions can be argued for and against, but throw up for us deep existential questions about how we define ourselves and others. How do we recognise 'otherness'? Is it external, psychological, physical, behavioural and so on?

In the past, there was not much of an acknowledged problem with diversity at a leadership level. There seemed to be little enthusiasm for diversification, with white, middle-aged, middle-class men generally recruiting other white, middle-aged and middle-class men to leadership positions. In this way, many leaders were safeguarded against their existential fear of uncertainty, at least at the surface level. With today's greater awareness of the need for equal opportunities, and with the growing understanding that diversity brings new ideas, essential to the lifeblood of any organisation, this is no longer an option.

On the whole, many people fear the unknown. Yet, one of the most pressing requirements of this century is the need to better understand and address the basic principles that relate to understanding each other, and acknowledge the legitimacy of other ways of knowing and being-in-the-world, which may not necessarily be consistent with or even similar to our own. Dealing with increased globalisation, how we understand ourselves, our interactions with others, our surroundings and our place in the universe takes centre stage for today's leader and calls for a consideration of where we and others sit within all the existential dimensions.

We cannot any longer afford to psychologically, physically and economically avoid engagement with the 'Cultural Other', which Sanderson (2004, p. 2) described as that *"awkward entity" which is increasingly projected into our midst as a result of global forces.'* We often feel the need to divide the world into those we believe are like us and those we perceive as being different from us. This latter group can be experienced as 'the Aliens', 'the They' or 'the Other'. The 'Other' may intrigue and excite us and we may wish to know more about them, or they may have an uncomfortably close connection with uncertainty – if they are not like me, how do I know what they will think, and, an even scarier prospect for many people, how do I know what they will do? In other words, the very existence of someone outwardly unlike me leads to the 'fear of the unknown'. We may apply these alienating terms to individuals, groups or even faceless transnational corporations, which may be experienced as a threat to the company or to individual economies. As Westbam (2002, p. 94 in Ali, 2002) points out, *'we come into the world with deep, gut fears…we fear the unknown, we fear the unfamiliar, and we are hostile to whatever we fear'.*

One of the challenges is how to respond to these nascent fears in the face of the increasingly omnipresent Cultural Other, given that our worldview (the way we in the West think about ourselves and Otherness) is not surprisingly mainly determined by our western ideology, ontology and epistemology. Said (1995, p. 334) saw the current position as presenting a challenge to the view of a *'supposedly stable binary opposition'* of a seemingly submissive East and a more dominant West. A leader has to take an existential view that by exploring the worldview of 'the Other' they will not only learn something about the Other but also about themselves. In acknowledging otherness, we are also acknowledging our relatedness and shining a spotlight on who we are. I only know the lightness of the day because I experience the darkness of the night; I only know I am a woman because there is such a thing as a man. I learn about myself through learning about others. If I encounter otherness with open, positive curiosity, the experience is likely to be a creative one, allowing me to experience new ways of thinking and doing things. It is upon the framework of creative change that businesses grow. If we work to sustain the otherness as a defence against uncertainty, then we are in danger of not just missing out on business opportunities but on a degree of self-knowledge which is hard to encounter elsewhere. *'It is manifestly clear that as much as we need to engage with ideas of Otherness, there is a necessity to disengage with one's own identity and self-reflect on its construction'* (Sanderson, 2004, p. 15). Existentialism presents the leader with the opportunity of developing a realistic and authentic account of the individual as an existent in a temporal, shifting and uncertain world.

If we really seek to introduce an existential approach into leadership challenges inherent in relatedness, we must question many aspects of current leadership behaviour. In addition to working sensitively and creatively with the 'Other', we must also challenge how we work with those we perceive as being 'like us'.

As a cautionary tale I can offer an experience of my own. On leaving my convent grammar school for girls to start a Fine Art degree, I was fearful about the 'Others' I might meet on my first day. I assumed they might be more experienced and worldly wise than me. On that first day I noticed another long-haired young woman whose Irish-originated surname was the same as mine apart from one letter. She was quiet, and in my mind I built a common narrative for the both of us – brought up Roman Catholic, convent educated, lacking in worldly experience and so on. We gravitated to each other. Over time I learnt we had very little in common. She had a three-year-old son and on becoming pregnant at 15 had been shipped off to Manchester to procure an abortion. She chose a different path, choosing a life as a single, unsupported mother, living in a bedsit. We both came from Roman Catholic families but she had not attended a convent school. I had been born and brought up in Manchester in a very supportive and liberal family. Despite our different prior experiences, we remained friends. It is so easy to perceive sameness or difference where it doesn't exist.

The challenge of temporality

The main existential challenge for all of us is to find a way of being with our temporal existence. Uncomfortable though this truth is, we are essentially beings-towards-death. Even thinking about this can send us headlong into ontological anxiety and despair, or it can remind us how precious every moment is and lead us to commit to living life to the full.

Just as we interpret everything in our world, we interpret time; we experience it differently in different contexts and in different stages of life. Remember back to how long a year seemed when as a child it was measured as the minutes between Christmas or our birthday and contrast it with the shock we feel when looking in our diaries as an adult and noting how quickly one year moves into another.

We cannot control time, and concerns about control and temporality are evident throughout business practice. Our desire to transcend and control death and our knowledge that this is not possible leads us to seek control over what we believe we *can* control. Leadership offers itself as a piece in this existential puzzle. It is a symbol of security, power and control for those who lead and for those who follow, and may even act as a buffer from addressing the reality of temporality. Five-year plans and endless strategies can lead us to pretend that there isn't an ending and that time will continue uninterrupted. All our experience shows this to be incorrect, and yet we may long to believe it.

No matter how important our leadership position is, there will come a day when we are no longer filling that role. We may have positively stepped away to take on different challenges or to move to something which carries more meaning for us. We may have involuntarily left the role through redundancy, redeployment, retirement, business closure, illness or death. This is equally true for everyone we are leading. An existential leader will hold at the forefront of their thoughts the importance of temporality and making the time we have meaningful. They will show sensitivity to its meaning for themselves and others.

As our time is limited, we are all required to carefully consider how we allocate it. Work procedures have had to change to allow for better work/life balance. As leaders we are faced with incorporating new ways of working which suit the more diverse and complex needs of a group of workers who are working longer, whilst balancing more commitments (as parents, carers, portfolio workers etc.) than previous generations.

We exist, and indeed we lead within the existential constraints of finitude and our human need for meaning and relationship. Given the temporality of our stay on this planet, it is essential that we consider our decisions and actions carefully and take responsibility for them. Given the knowledge of the temporality of our state, the significance of the choices we make becomes greater over time, particularly when we are taking on a leadership role where our decisions can have a major impact on the lives of others.

The challenge of meaning-making

Existential leadership offers a new vision, based on coherence and meaning; harmonious understanding of shared concerns – freedom, meaning, aloneness, death; a common reality with a concurrent vision and consideration of social/ ethical/knowledge/environmental elements. Work can be experienced as a place to find meaning. We will be in relation to others, and by using the freedom to determine how we encounter and be with others we are offered the opportunity to learn more about ourselves, opening up a more diverse set of possibilities as potential pathways to meaning. Leaders offer up one aspect of meaning through their vision and the values and beliefs underpinning that vision. This needs to be translated into action which is congruent and aligned to their values and meaning.

Nietzsche (1998, p. 6) reminds us that, *'If you have your why? for life, then you can get along with almost any how?'* If employees can *'achieve a sense of coherence, a sense that work is more than just productivity, that work also generates meaning'* (Schultz, 2004, p. 24), then whatever the nature of their work, it can address an existential need to find meaning in daily life. Indeed, it could be argued that instilling meaning and purpose in an organisation is a leader's main task from which all other leadership skills flow. For a workplace to hold meaning-making at its heart requires robust existential leadership.

To work existentially, a leader is required not just to adopt a set of behaviours, but also to embrace a philosophical approach, a 'way of being' which calls on the leader to not just 'behave' but to 'be' different. It is not enough to set people tasks and leave them to it. This sets them in motion, but motion focuses on behaviours and actions, whilst emotion focuses on passion and meaning. It could be said that motion is what we do and emotion is why we do it. Motion can get things done when the leader is present, but emotion, passion and commitment can sustain behaviour in the leader's absence. Leaders in motion differ from leaders who connect with emotion, with the latter understanding their role as what we call 'meaning makers'. Drath and Palus (1994, p. 13) describe meaning-making as an activity which constructs *a sense of what is, what actually exists, and, of that, what is important*. They believe that people construct this for themselves, yet that *people also construct with others, together, a socially oriented sense of what is and what is important. When this happens in association with practice (work)...we say that the process of leadership is happening*. As we have seen in considering temporality, this need for meaning is not just a matter of concern for leaders themselves, but equally to their followers. Leaders must therefore creatively manage the fusion of individualised and organisational meaning.

An existential leader will be willing to 'go deeper' in their approach and specifically in their relationship to others through their own search for meaning and their attempts to understand what is meaningful for others. This requires the existential leader to first reflect on what constitutes their own meaning. The psychologist Wendy Ulrich and the organisation theorist Dave Ulrich (2010) propose seven questions which a meaning maker will ask of themselves:

- Who am I?
- Where am I going?
- Whom do I travel with?
- How do I build a positive work environment?
- How do I change learn and grow
- What challenges interest me?
- What delights me?

These questions can be easily mapped onto the existential dimensions, personal, psychological, physical and spiritual, and be linked to the big existential concerns of relatedness, authenticity, freedom and responsibility, uncertainty and temporality.

Writers such as Flores and colleagues see the whole meaning of business itself as having shifted from task oriented to meaning oriented. Segal (2004, p. 40) reflects that *business used to be seen as a rational activity aimed at the satisfaction of desires* but is now seen as *a form of disclosing new worlds* and therefore in the business of meaning-making. Rickards and Murray (2006, p. 24) believe that leaders must be engaged with making meaning but also with the management of meaning and point to phenomenology (although they never name it) as a way of understanding this, *'to understand such a leadership style, we have to accept that we are entering the world of perceptions, and beliefs, often dismissed as "soft" and subjective'*. Kets de Vries (2003, p. xv), too, points out that we need to move away from *'rational approaches to management, which assume that human beings can be managed solely by logical, means-to-an-end modes of organization...as corporate executives, like the rest of us, are not always rational beings; they may be driven by emotions, aspirations or fantasies that influence the way they run their companies on a day-to-day basis.'* An approach based on phenomenology and existentialism is not seeking to fit with what is considered rational.

It may be possible to find life-expanding meaningful experiences in work which will, to some degree, deaden our existential fear and allow us to leave something permanent, transcending our mortal death. An existential leader remains alert to the need for work to be meaningful and will provide meaningful opportunities based on this belief.

The challenge of values and beliefs

Holding and reflecting on our values and beliefs is an important part of the existential approach. In considering the challenge of meaning, I have linked values and beliefs to meaning-making. It is hard to imagine how anything can be meaningful if it does not fit with one's values. The values I hold as leader, and the values of my followers, are fundamental to who we are. If I live an existence which is not consistent with my values, I am living inauthentically and therefore uncomfortably. Many of our behaviours stem from our underlying values and beliefs.

If we are to understand and work effectively with others, it is essential that we understand a person's values. If we wish to motivate people, a key requirement of any leader, we have to appeal to their values. In crude terms, a person whose values are financial will respond well to offers of a pay increase, whilst another who is primarily motivated by meaning will respond better to the offer of more meaningful work challenges.

As we are motivated by our own values, we need to take care to consider that these values may not be shared with others. Our values are so important to us as individuals that we tend to believe that they are best, not just for us, but also for everyone else. If we find something works for us, or excites us, we tend to believe the same will be true for others. Some leaders act as though this were the case and so fail to take heed of all inconsistency between company, leader and staff values. As leaders we must remember the existential belief in the uniqueness of each individual whilst sharing a set of existential givens (i.e. those things which as humans we all share – death, temporality, anxiety, need to be heard, search for meaning, isolation). When I learn something about myself, I would be wrong to assume that I have learnt something which is a given in human nature. What I have learnt is something which sits well with me as an individual and with my values.

The desire to win provides an excellent example. Although competitive people like to win, many others dislike judging or being judged and are demotivated by competition because it is opposed to their values. Not to understand and work with this will make poor leaders who do not help their 'followers' achieve their full potential. It will also prevent the company from achieving its potential. A safe environment where values and behaviours can be openly questioned and explored is a fertile soil for creativity. An atmosphere which closes down debate and disagreement is missing out on the potential for exciting new developments. A leader who is authentic and has a robust sense of self and self-worth (very different from arrogance) is not threatened by different values and disagreements but encourages difference which is openly and positively shared. An existential leader will seek to identify and work with the values of team members. This helps build a coherent and collaborative team.

Equally, the team will look to the company to demonstrate a set of organisational values which they can 'sign up to'. These values are first signalled in the company's vision statement. For many companies these values are prompted by market needs and so often lack any existential depth. Schultz (2004, p. 123) suggests that employees will often try to *duplicate this set of values in order to adapt'*, but in doing so lose *'touch with their own identities, creating "existential pain and doubt"'*.

To provide a set of values which are mutually meaningful for the leader, the organisation and the employees requires leaders to know their employees not just on a performance level but also on a personal level. This carries *'a very direct responsibility for being existentially present for their employees, for being able to take up the big questions with them, for being able to make the workplace a framework for something existential'* (Schultz, 2004, p. 46). Of course, leaders may have thousands of employees and cannot be expected to know each of them. Leaders must look to their team leaders and managers to keep them aware of the concerns of individuals. In a leadership post in which I carried responsibility for a very large number of people, I found that monthly coffee mornings with union leaders also helped me to be aware of employees' needs and values and to what extent the organisation was serving these. These mornings were well worth the time investment as I was able to quickly pick up and resolve concerns.

As a leader, I may have to contend with a clash of values, not just between others and myself, but also between conflicting values of my own. I remember a time when I was forced to prioritise between my values. A relatively new member of my senior management team appeared to be making little or no progress on specific tasks which were discussed weekly. When I enquired why this was, he informed me that there was nothing I had *instructed* him to do and so he 'had not failed to do anything he had been asked to'. This was technically correct. I had laid out the direction of travel, the desired milestones and deadlines, but had never said you must do A, B or C. So, I was presented with a dilemma. My leadership style was that, within defined boundaries, I would invest a lot of autonomy in my senior managers, expecting that they would welcome the potential for creativity and the opportunity to bring something of their own to the outcome. One of my strong values was to empower my team by not micromanaging whilst being clear about what was required of them and the time by which outcomes had to be achieved. I left the 'how' very much open to the individual's creativity. I did not mind when or where they worked. If it was at home in the garden with a glass of wine, this was not a problem, as long as they delivered quality work to the agreed deadline. At the same time I held the equally strong value that the service we provided to clients was paramount and needed to be excellent and on time.

Here I was faced with an individual with a very different worldview to my own. He was first in the office in the morning and often last to leave but I was unsure what happened between those two events! It seemed that in this instance I could not hold true to both my values equally. If I required good service I needed to manage in a different style from my usual transformational approach. I did not want to tell a senior manager how or when to move from one small step to another but equally I did not want to let clients down by failing to deliver an excellent service. I openly discussed this personal dilemma with the manager and checked that he really did want detailed task management. I explained that it did not sit well with my leadership values, but that if it was what he wanted and needed then I would do so in order not to fail the client. I also needed to be clear with him that I would not be managing anyone else in that way and voiced my concern that this micromanagement was inappropriate to his status, and therefore could be experienced as condescending. It was important to me to share all these aspects with him in order to remain authentic.

Following our conversation, he requested that he be given step-by-step directions and so we signed an agreement to that effect. I felt the need for the written agreement as micromanagement can be seen as bullying or harassment, and indeed that is how I would have experienced it if I had been on the receiving end. Despite being given detailed instructions, his work did not improve, but at least I felt I had listened and attempted to work within his worldview. Shortly after, he left the company.

An organisation with clear and congruent values and beliefs, consistently demonstrated by organisational ethos and behaviours, is a strong organisation. Schultz (2004, p. 131) states that, *'Existentially strong companies and managers find their values and stand by them, regardless of how others react; and existentially strong employees do precisely the same, even when they separate them from all other employees'*.

The challenge of uncertainty

Uncertainty sits very closely alongside temporality, with death providing the final challenge in uncertainty. By letting go of certainty we are not embracing an unbearable state of uncertainty but welcoming openness, curiosity and a willingness to embrace paradox and creativity.

Life is uncertain in its meaning, uncertain in its future and uncertain because there exists no certainty beyond the finite nature of our existence. So it is only deluded leaders who believe they can control things and defeat uncertainty by creating organizational charts, five-year plans and complex strategic documents. All of these things may give people a false and limited sense of 'certainty', but it is merely a temporary comforting mirage. There is nothing wrong with providing temporal limited 'certainty'. It would be impossible to live life if we did not choose to consider that some things carry a high degree of certainty. Structures and plans are needed in business to measure development and success, but they guarantee nothing. They are mere hopes and aspirations, and no matter how well thought out they are, considered against a realistic risk assessment and knowledge of the organisation and the market, they are by no means 'certain'. However, existentially strategic plans do provide a canvas on which to write large the leader's values and those of the organisation. They can provide a vision of the company's intentions and hopes.

Whether we seek it or not, followers will look to leaders for certainty. Organised religions, cults, groups, gurus and the like are attractive because they claim to hold some truth. We are led to believe that if we accept their truth and follow certain paths there will be some type of guaranteed and certain result. For some leaders, taking on the mantle of the 'truth holder' or 'guru' is welcomed as a way of bringing recognition of their power, a sign of respect and sublimation. It can feel seductive. It may seem hard to acknowledge that as a leader you have doubts and that you cannot guarantee anything. Not to acknowledge this truth is to be inauthentic and yet does this mean that as a leader I need to burden my followers by sharing all the uncertainty I feel? The answer to this will lie in your values and the way you relate to your followers and must be set in the context in which you are operating.

The challenge of authenticity

Having earlier looked at leadership styles for this century, I have drawn attention to the move towards Authentic Leadership, which as we have seen has its champions and its detractors. It is not enough to talk about authenticity; it requires doing and being. The word 'authentic' derives from the Greek meaning 'one who accomplishes'. To be authentic is to accomplish in the world and to make choices that have consequences out in the world. This could equally stand as a definition of leadership. It is not just the making of the decisions that is important in this context, but 'how' the choices are made and how leaders manifest these choices ontologically.

To be true to oneself, one has to be self aware and continually reflect on and challenge one's self-concept. Such critical self-reflection helps leaders to know themselves and gain clarity and concordance in relation to their core values, beliefs, identity, emotions, goals and motives. These elements are not static, hence the challenge to continually check on them and ensure they do not become sedimented. The consideration of these factors allows for authentic action without limiting possibilities. It does not make the choices easier. A leader may still have to choose between making people redundant or allowing the company to fold. One can choose to take that action authentically and honestly, or not. One has to be willing to critically self-examine one's motivations and actions.

The leader's openness to self-criticism and commitment to being honest inspire trust in those looking to them for leadership. No one can be truly and consistently authentic; it is an ideal to be aimed for and everyone behaves inauthentically at times, saying and doing things they will come to regret. The key is to have the self-awareness to recognise these times and to take feedback well.

Often leaders and others are confused about what authentic behaviour is, and imagine that it always means saying what you think. However, it is important to consider *how* things are said. Honesty is important, but it can be brutal, even bullying. Authentic leaders are sensitive and demonstrate an authentic, consistently congruent connection between their values and their behaviours. Perhaps the greatest challenge of authentic leadership is to relinquish the impulse to dominate others, an impulse often present in leaders and often associated with the role. Authenticity calls for a truthful alignment between what you think, say and do as a leader.

The challenge of freedom

Leaders are usually appointed to make decisions on the part of an organisation, company or group. It is assumed that leadership brings the freedom to make such decisions, the power to make them happen and the willingness to take responsibility for the outcomes.

We have seen how central the concept of freedom is in existential thought. Kierkegaard often reminds us, in many of his writings, that by daring to engage with our freedom we risk losing our foothold momentarily, but that in failing to engage at all, we risk losing ourselves totally.

We may not feel free, yet we cannot escape from the fact that we are free. Indeed, when I have been in a leadership role, the apparent freedom invested in the role has, at times, seemed illusionary. The responsibility, however, has felt very real indeed.

Any decision we make, even one *not* to make a decision, is a choice flowing from our freedom to chose. As Kierkegaard described it, freedom is experienced as a kind of 'dizziness', which in itself causes anxiety. Although we are free, we obviously make our choices within the perceived constraints of our context and with the view to the possible implications of the choice. Every decision we make brings gains and losses, and we must decide what we can bear to lose and what we can't.

One way in which we seek to avoid the giddiness of the responsibility embodied in freedom is to look to pass that freedom, power and responsibility on to someone else. A leader provides the perfect receptacle for the anxiety freedom creates, and so we tend to look to leaders to provide us with a perceived defence against our existential freedom. They can be experienced as providing the belief or hope that if there is someone 'above' me making the decisions, I can live in denial of my own freedom to decide. It is the decision-maker that carries the blame if things go wrong, and they provide the perfect mechanism for absorbing any guilt. So, people may see leaders as a type of human shield behind which they can hide. They desire the leader to provide structure, to offset responsibility and to safeguard them from their freedom by 'seemingly' limiting their choices.

However, things are changing. More leaders are allowing employees autonomy as they integrate their home and work lives. In business, freedom can be seen as a blessing and/or a curse. If we encourage, or merely allow, employees a degree of freedom, we can encourage creativity and a sense of responsibility and ownership, but for some leaders this is a very frightening prospect. Indeed, for some employees, too, this is a challenge too far. To be free may feel liberating, but it is often not comfortable, because freedom creates anxiety. Giving freedom and responsibility to others may require the leader to encourage, or even push, people out of their comfort zone, increasing their trust in themselves as a response to the trust a leader is placing in them.

If as a leader I offer a level of freedom to my team and encourage them to express their thoughts, both positive and negative, I must then face the challenge of remaining authentic to my commitment to participation, and so debate and act appropriately on what I hear. I am sure most of you have been through company consultation exercises where you have known that any decisions have already been taken and that whatever you say is just a PR nod to the need to be seen as a participative organisation. Little deflates morale and trust more quickly than feeling used in that way.

It can be difficult to define what exactly freedom means and yet it can be equally challenging, and paradoxical, to define its boundaries. In the workplace, giving employees the room to reach their objectives in the ways they see fit can be a solid leadership move, if done correctly. Freedom in the workplace can include the ability to keep nontraditional hours, work from home, take unlimited vacation days, exercise creativity in how to approach immediate job goals or otherwise. New technology means that leaders may see little of staff who may work remotely. Leaders must know what they will do if the employee chooses to use their freedom to do something in a way which does not fit with their expectations. For many leaders delegation is a challenge, as is resisting the desire to meddle in the work others are undertaking. This disempowers them and they will quickly realise that the freedom offered is severely limited and inauthentic, potentially causing them to lose trust in the leader.

If a leader is willing to take up the challenge of increasing the freedom offered to others, they can benefit through the increased creativity resulting from the freedom to experiment and get it wrong. If people feel that they can make some choices on the job, they are more likely to 'own' the work and take responsibility for the outcome. If the leader invests in training and developing people, then it will only frustrate them if they are not given the freedom to try out their new learning. It would also represent money poorly invested by the leader.

The challenge of our emotional being

Past generations of leaders would never have considered that there was a place for emotions in the business world. The transactional approach, particularly in the military, was aimed at taking emotions out of the leadership relationship. It dealt with the unquestioned undertaking of tasks, without any emotional reaction or commitment, which were often considered signs of weakness. It is understandable that in military action when lives are at risk, it may be life threatening to stop, feel and reflect when your enemy has a weapon targeted on you. Quick, unreflected and 'unemotional' action can save lives. It can also allow people to drop bombs without feeling any emotional connection in the present to the impact of the action on fellow human beings now referred to as 'collateral damage' to remove us even further from emotional connection. The suppressed emotions may of course resurface many months or even years later, as post-traumatic shock. We have heard horrific stories from the world wars of very young men who were unable to suppress natural emotional responses to situations and were executed as cowards. Fortunately, with increased recognition of battlefield and post-traumatic stress, we are better placed to understand and validate emotional reactions to testing or stimulating events, and military training now reflects that human beings are emotional by their very nature. Emotion signifies connection, and we now understand that to connect to anything with a passion is an emotional commitment. Leaders look for passion and commitment, and so we have seen the growing acceptance of the importance of emotional intelligence in the world of work.

Acknowledging and welcoming emotions is not about being 'warm and fluffy'. All emotions are intentional. They do not exist in isolation. They are caused by something and are directed at something or somebody. For example, I feel angry because something has happened to make me feel angry, and my anger will be directed at the organisation or the person (it could be myself) who carried out, or failed to carry out, a particular action. As a leader it is time well invested if I seek to find the intentionality of an emotion, instead of trying to close the emotion down or to assume that I know the reason for it.

People have different emotional responses to different things because 'things' are imbued with different meanings for each of us. If I hear that someone's dog has died, being a dog lover, I will feel sad and think about the desolation I have felt when pets have died. I may start to offer condolences, only to discover that the dog was bad tempered and out of control and had severely mauled the person's child. I need to hold back my assumptions and listen to the emotional experience of the other person.

Emotions are not simple. They can be paradoxical, with us holding opposing emotions at the same time. I am sure we have all experienced those conflicting emotions of love and hate when someone we love does something to hurt us. In business a person could feel relieved that they have not been given a difficult task to do whilst at they same time they may feel disrespected and angry, believing that the leader did not consider that they could do the task.

If I am an emotionally intelligent leader, then I know that human beings are not rational creatures. I will seek out ambiguities, not as a way to catch someone out, but to show that I grasp the complexity of the event and the emotional reaction to it. In the case above I may discover that a person needs support to increase their self-confidence.

In this chapter I have drawn attention to the philosophical challenges a leader faces. In part II I aim to show how this philosophical approach, based on existential principles, can serve as a framework for addressing some of the more practical challenges in leadership.

Any project, be it professional or personal, starts with an idea or a goal. The goal does not have to be big or dramatic; it may just be a decision to pass time in a meaningful way. It is, however, based on a concrete decision to commit to something, even if only for a few minutes, as in a daily 10-minute meditation session. As we can see, the previous two sentences embody some important existential aspects – meaning, time, freedom and responsibility.

The decision to embark on a project comes from a vision, which is where most businesses or organisations start. A business vision must speak to existential, as well as business, needs. For this reason I intend to start the next section by exploring how existential ideas can help to form a business vision.

Part II

Working practically with the existential leadership approach

In Part I, I took you speedily through the essential elements which make a person into a 'Leader'. I set this in the context of various leadership theories. From there I proceeded to explore what we understand by the term 'Existential', drawing on writers such as Kierkegaard, Nietzsche, Heidegger, Jaspers, Marcel, de Beauvoir, Merleau-Ponty, Camus and Sartre, amongst others. Finally, in Part I, we looked at what this century, with its growing focus on living with uncertainty, needs from its leaders, and proposed that an existential approach addresses some, if not all, of these needs.

So far, I have focused on philosophy, past studies and research into leadership approaches, and have thus remained in mainly theoretical territory. I have already expressed how important it is to me that we apply and test theoretical assumptions in everyday contexts. This second part of the book attempts to set leadership theories and existential philosophy in an applied business context. Leaders have a great many leadership challenges and it is impossible to address them all, so I have chosen to consider how three major challenges, which all leaders will face at some time, can be approached in a very practical way by drawing on existential concepts and phenomenological approaches.

Any project, business or organisation starts with a vision. It may be a value-led vision, which aims to change something for the better, or may be a vision in which the visionary is primarily concerned with personal or organisational material gain. On a personal level this may focus on gains in identity, purpose, finances and power. Organisationally it may be concerned with changes based on philosophical or political aims. The two are not incompatible and may happily coexist, but a vision is likely to favour one aim above the other. Any vision is an attempt, at some level, to address the anxiety of uncertainty by seeking to offer something clear and concrete. As the vision is so important in setting out the core concerns of the business, I would suggest that it is basically existential in nature, addressing issues or organisational values and beliefs, the extent and limitation of freedoms and offering an authentic framework on which to support growth and creativity. I have looked to some existing visions and identified existential themes within them, as well as laying out what a vision maker may wish to consider in drawing up an existentially informed vision.

Once the vision is established, a leader moves on to the implementation of that vision. A leader cannot usually implement their vision alone. They need to recruit, retain and develop others who will engage with them in making their vision a reality. For this reason I move my focus from the place of existential thought in the forming of a vision to using human resources to make the vision happen. I aim to show that in bringing existential considerations into play in the recruitment, retention and development of its staff, an organisation heightens its chances of being a successful operation. It is more likely to recruit staff who are aligned to the values and philosophy of its vision, and therefore passionately committed to making it a reality and so willing to embrace any developmental needs which may prove necessary. In this section I include a consideration of existential elements in training and coaching.

Finally, in this part of the book, I look at managing conflict. All leaders will encounter conflict. Indeed, creativity requires a level of conflict or we would remain with the status quo. I propose a creative existential approach to conflict management and resolution, which I have found to be very successful in my roles as leader, manager or mediator. This includes an introduction to the process of existentially informed mediation.

Chapter 5

An existential approach to creating, communicating and implementing a vision

Whether it is formalised or not, anyone starting a company will have a vision of how they want that company to be and what they want to achieve. Even though Kelly (1998) warns us that corporate life is complex and to some extent crazy and any belief that a business can be reduced to an organisational chart is merely window dressing, businesses continue to believe that they can create linear plans and complex structural charts based on a company vision. Despite Kelly's warning and lots of evidence that such systems and structures may achieve very little, a company does still need a vision to address a number of existential needs.

It is a central task of a leader to inspire others. A leader needs to create an inspiring vision, hopefully in collaboration with others, but also be open to regularly deconstructing, and possibly destroying, that vision. If we become stuck, or sedimented, within a vision, we can lose our potential for creativity. We can become absorbed in one set of conventions and ways of being and thus find it impossible to experience that there are other ways of seeing things. Segal (2004) sees it as a similar experience to being in Plato's cave. In *The Republic*, Plato offers us the 'Allegory of the Cave' in which he asks us to, *'See human beings as though they were in an underground cave-like dwelling with its entrance, a long one, open to the light across the whole width of the cave. They are in it from childhood with their legs and necks in bonds so that they are fixed, seeing only in front of them, unable because of the bond to turn their head all the way around'* (trans. Bloom, 1968, p. 193). Their viewpoint is fixed. There are a number of people walking past the entrance to the cave, but those in the cave can only see their shadows projected onto the wall. As this is all they see, they believe the images to be the real thing rather than a shadow. For them, this is the insubstantial reality of their world. When they are unchained and free to turn and look, they find things are very different, richer and more complex, and their understanding of the world is thrown into question. An inflexible and unreflected-upon vision can be like staring at Plato's cave wall and believing that one knows all there is to know. A limited perspective will not create a vision which is fit for purpose. Drucker (1997) echoes this, claiming that every business holds an implicit theory and set of beliefs about the world. This can prevent the leader from seeing things in any other way. The leader is often unaware of how this set of beliefs is operating and controlling them by shaping and limiting their business. This sedimentation is particularly dangerous in a time of change. Drucker calls for a conscious 'abandoning' of these theories, recommending that, *'Every three years, an organisation should challenge every product, every service, every policy, every distribution channel with the question, if we were not in it already, would we be going into it now?'* (1997, p. 44).

A leader needs to build a vision capable of flex and change. The idea that we can merely create the vision then rest is a false one. The vision must be regularly reviewed and, if necessary, amended. This is in tune with Heidegger's process of 'destruction', which calls for an open and passionate contextual drilling down of embodied thought. It can be articulated as 'convention-disruption-vision', a concept further developed by the marketing expert Jean Marie Dru to help companies continually reassess and change their products and brands. This is not a one-off activity and should not be seen as chronological or linear, but as a renewing circular process. Today's visionary CEOs and entrepreneurs, working with new ways of working, new technologies and globalisation, understand this. They recognise that businesses are more than just a means to an end. For many people, their identities are tightly woven into their work, and an organisation has to repeatedly reinvent itself for it to retain meaning. Flores and Letelier (2013) saw the enduring and essential feature of the industrial era as being the capacity to invent new worlds. The first step in that invention is to envisage it and to convey that vision to others.

In this way, the vision is reassessed; we look up from the wall towards the cave entrance and see the light. Leaders must continually disrupt sedimented thinking, staid habits and conventions, and create new visions fit for their time. Schumpeter (1950, p. 118) introduced existential language into the understanding of capitalism, understanding the angst present in business and the embodied and spiritual impact this may have on leaders. In his entrepreneurial philosophy, with its concept of creative destruction (also known as Schumpeter's gale), which he describes as *'the process of industrial mutation that incessantly revolutionizes the economic structure from within, incessantly destroying the old one, incessantly creating a new one'*, progress is seen to require a series of self-generated destruction activities leading to reconfigurations. It is like being swept along by a gale and not knowing where one will end up. This is a truth which is necessary to hold in mind when building, agreeing and reviewing a vision. Foster and Kaplan (2001) warn of the dangers of 'cultural lock-in' where the assumptions of leaders make it impossible to change the corporate culture, even in the face of clear market threats and changing environment. The 'stuckness' or 'sedimentation' which ensues, will no doubt be met with the cooling of passion, as people lose touch with the meaning they originally identified with in the vision.

In creating a new vision, a leader must honestly explore the assumptions they are holding about the 'why' of the work (its meaning and relevance) and the 'how' of the work (business practises). Grint (1995, 2005) called for a process of 'defamiliarization' in which we are called upon to examine the present in the light of both potential and plural alternatives. This is in line with the phenomenological approach in which all assumptions are 'bracketed'.

Despite the warnings of being potentially 'trapped' by a vision, I still believe it is important to have one, in order to address a number of existential needs. Existential, Connective and other leadership theories have shown how an increasing number of workers at all levels look to work to provide meaning. Work occupies much of a person's life and so they may seek to meet some of their existential needs in the workplace. One way to access meaning is through a corporate vision which can be understood and connected with and is consistent with the people's values and beliefs. Of course, if a person's core value is to provide financially for their family, the nature of the work may be less significant than the remuneration it provides.

The search for meaning is an existential given, a spiritual search for purpose in our existence, for understanding how our life events (including work) fit into a larger context. Meaning in life is a spiritual quest to find a reason for 'being' and to feel that this 'being' has significance. It relates to a sense of fulfilling a higher purpose that results in a higher significance than just surviving. We want to feel that we have made, or are able to make, a difference in the world.

The search for life meaning is a core element of spirituality, which lies at the heart of the existential dimension of Uberwelt. Spirituality should not be equated with religion; spirituality encompasses far more. It is concerned with seeking fulfilment and a feeling of connectedness with others and with the cosmos. It asks such questions as 'What is important enough for me to die for', 'What is essential to my existence?', 'What makes my life worth living?', 'What are the conditions under which I experience my life as meaningful?' or 'How does my work contribute to making my life meaningful?'

We bring our spiritual selves to work and much of our spiritual odyssey occurs within the context of the workplace. Because work is a central part of human existence, we seek for ways to connect our working lives with our spiritual lives. However, the importance and relevance of life meaning is mostly structurally ignored in the workplace. This is probably because the eternal quest for the 'meaning of life' is regarded as too philosophical and not relevant to the harsh realities of the competitive world of work.

Frankl, a Jewish psychiatrist, Nazi concentration camp survivor, and author of the acclaimed *Man's Search for Meaning*, argued that the essence of human motivation is the 'will to meaning', a striving to find and realise meaning in life. He reasoned that there is nothing that so effectively helps people to survive even the worst conditions as the knowledge that there is a purpose in life. Research in psychiatry and clinical psychology supports Frankl's views, confirming with overwhelming consistency that a sense of meaning is an important correlate of mental and psychological health. Higher levels of meaning have been found to correlate positively with self-esteem, control, life satisfaction, engagement, a generous attitude towards others and positive attitudes. In contrast, lack of life meaning (meaninglessness) has been found to correlate with a lack of well-being and with psychopathology in a roughly linear way. Lack of meaning can manifest in loss of social identity, social isolation, substance abuse, suicidal ideation, neuroticism and anxiety. Particular groups of people, such as prison inmates and schizophrenic patients, are considered to experience less meaning than people in general. These findings show that meaning relates to almost every component of well-being with only slight variations in the strength of the associations. So it is to be expected that having a sense of life meaning has an important influence on positive work attitudes and outcomes.

Indeed, there is a rapidly increasing body of research that confirms that spirituality in general, and life meaning specifically, influence positive work outcomes and attitudes significantly. People who have a higher sense of meaning show more commitment towards their careers and are more willing to make significant career changes to align their work with their sense of meaning. As a result, they experience more career satisfaction and career progress. They are even willing and eager to continue to work in the absence of financial necessity. However, a sense of meaning does not result in commitment that is forced or unbalanced – for instance sacrificing themselves for their work, or allowing work to dominate their lives. People with a higher sense of life meaning are more content and understand the importance and necessity to make time for healthy introspection. They generally tend to lead healthier and more balanced lifestyles. Similarly, people having a sense of meaning are more altruistic and less selfish, focusing outside themselves and attending to the plight of others. They may also be more motivated. Intrinsic motivation stems from a deeper psychological level than is often acknowledged. This is important, as we know that the most powerful predictor of job satisfaction is intrinsic motivation, not the other way around. Work satisfaction and life meaning go together. A sense of meaning in life provides the motivation to execute our daily work, even if the work itself does not particularly stimulate us. Meaning in life effectively contributes towards goal orientation that supports willingness to learn new things and to attempt goals with a high possibility of failure.

We cannot ignore the important role that meaning in life has in the workplace. We attach meanings to work beyond that of economic utility. We want to see a larger purpose in our work. Most external methods we apply in our attempts to motivate people are in vain unless they also enhance a sense of meaning in people's existence or meaningfulness in the tasks that they are responsible for.

Our workplaces are spiritual places. Business education and leadership have a spiritual tone that we are not always aware of, yet cannot ignore. Our task as leaders exists on a much deeper level of spiritual interaction with subordinates than is often anticipated. Similarly, as educators, we need to connect on a deeper spiritual level with students than we often do in business and leadership courses. In addition to everything else we do, we have a duty to assist people on their journey to find meaning in their existence; we need to enable them to a find and fulfil a higher life purpose through their work. A company needs an inspiring and meaningful vision which gives purpose and meaning to all its business activities, through all levels in the company.

An existential vision statement

So, when a business draws up its vision, it needs to take into account the universal need for meaning. A vision statement is a company's declaration of meaning. It is a road map which indicates what the company wants to become, is inspired by its values and beliefs and provides a guiding direction for the company's growth. For some companies, the creation of the vision statement is completed before the company is registered or staff appointments are made. For others the vision is cocreated with the employees, but those employees needed some kind of vision to inspire them to join in the journey in the first place. It is generally considered that to be effective, a vision statement must be:

- **Values based:** Demonstrates the values that are required to support the organisation.
- **Inspiring:** Is appealing enough to engage people to commit to a cause.
- **Future focused:** Indicates the 'big picture' and clearly describes what the organisation will be like in the future.
- **Directional:** Serves as guide to organisational plans and strategies.
- **Specific:** Is clear and focused enough to shape decision-making.
- **Relevant and purpose driven:** Reflects the company's response to the challenges of the day.
- **Challenging:** Inspires members of the organisation to do great things and achieve a higher level of standards.
- **Unique and memorable:** Highlights what makes the organisation different and why it matters.

Some vision statements are short yet manage to express the ethos of the company in a few words. I looked for examples of vision statements and by chance one of the first to appear was for Southwest Air. This made me decide to look to other examples within the airline industry. Here are four examples, all from airlines:

> *'To become the world's most loved, most flown, and most profitable airline'.*
>
> Southwest Air

> *'...working as one team to create memories our customers will want to talk to their families about.'*
>
> Jet2

> *'To offer low fares that generate increased passenger traffic while maintaining a continuous focus on cost containment and efficiency operation'.*
>
> Ryanair

> *'To embrace the human spirit and let it fly'.*
>
> Virgin Atlantic

We can see that even in these short statements we gain a glimpse into what the company's priorities and values are. The first two are primarily relational.

Southwest Air starts with customer satisfaction, being *'loved'*, and then moves on to economic profitability. Jet2 is the most relational, starting with the indication that its workforce is important in organisational success, working together as *'one team'* to achieve this, focusing on the customer experience through showing an understanding that their customers are part of the wider community with families and friends. This portrays the company as friendly and confident that it will be profitable by way of customer satisfaction and word of mouth recommendations. Ryanair, are not relational, customers are *'increased...traffic'* and the focus is on cost and efficiency. Virgin Atlantic bring a different approach; there is no talk of customers or profits, but a focus on the overall dream. It is focused on the 'big picture': *'embrace the human spirit'*, and tells us a lot about the hopes, passion and dreams of its founder, Richard Branson (whose image accompanies the statement), and by implication offers the invitation to join if you share these passions.

Using the existential components to create the vision

There are a number of common models for creating a vision statement. If we look at just one, the McKinsey 7-S model, we see that it offers seven interdependent factors which are categorised as either 'hard' or 'soft' elements. Hard elements are easier to define or identify, and management can directly influence them. They are made up of strategy statements, organisational charts and reporting lines, formal processes and IT systems. The soft elements can be more difficult to describe and are less tangible. Yet it is through these soft elements that the business will succeed or die. Within the soft elements are **'shared values'**, which were referred to as 'superordinate goals' when the model was first developed. These are the core values of the company as evidenced through the corporate culture and the generic work ethic. The leader creates, or at least cocreates, this value-led company ethos.

Some years ago, when I took up a leadership position in a large company, I noticed that their strong corporate values were tied to time keeping, or indeed to working unpaid overtime. Kudos was gained by the length of time your car sat in the car park, which was overlooked by the directors' office suite. Those arriving earliest and staying late were the ones who gained bonuses and promotions. When I analysed the successful output of the staff, it was not the 'long stay car parkers' who achieved most or who were most efficient. They did, however, drink the most coffee and use the internet for social media more than most! This did not fit with my values or what I wanted the company values to be. I wanted people to be in the office when they needed to be in order to produce high-quality work in time for necessary and realistic deadlines, to be free to use social media when time allowed and to be free to go home and work from there if appropriate. It did not matter to me where or when the work was done as long as it was done and done well. I started by role modelling this myself, emailing round to say that I would leave the office each day at 5 p.m. unless there were unforeseen circumstances. When people began to work in this way, productivity and job satisfaction increased.

Some value-led examples

In researching for this book, I randomly searched to see to what extent some companies' vision statements openly express an existential approach, even though they may not use the term 'existential'. I decided to start with Jet2, whose mission statement I have already referred to and which clearly shows a focus on the existential concern of relatedness in their values. I followed this up by looking at Innocent, where I would have expected to find a company led by values, and which was perhaps surprisingly sold to Coca-Cola in 2013.

Jet2 shows its values on its website for anyone looking for a job with the company. They are the first things shown before location, pay and benefits and so show the importance the company places on values. By implication, the company is looking for candidates who share these values. It expands on the short statement given earlier and divides its intentions into four areas,

- **Create memories**
  - We're here to Create Memories for our customers, from ensuring a swift and safe journey, right down to the little details that mean so much.
  - And we make working here a memorable experience for each other too. We're proud to be friendly, approachable, open and honest.
- **Be present**
  - We're always aware of what's going on around us, both in and out of the workplace. Whether that's comforting a nervous customer, welcoming a new colleague on board or asking one of our customers if they need a hand.
  - We're always present and every colleague is empowered to use their initiative to inspire others.
- **Work as one team**
  - We're working together to deliver that amazing journey to millions of customers, from customer facing roles on the ground and in the air, to all the behind the scenes activities that keep our customers happy and ensure our growth and success.
  - We couldn't do it without our people. We are proud to be One Team.
- **Take responsibility**
  - We always think about what we do and how this impacts both our customers and colleagues.
  - We empower our colleagues to take responsibility, and if there's a problem, we find a solution. If there's something we can do better, we do it.

If we consider these aspirational statements in relation to existential issues, what do we find? Probably the first thing we notice is the **relational** nature of all the statements. In existential thought there is considerable importance given to the knowledge that we are 'beings-in-the-world-with-others'. I doubt that Jet2 spent time reading and considering existential philosophy before determining its vision, but it may have interested the writers to know that Heidegger (1889–1976) proposed that as humans we live in a world which is primarily a 'with-world' where we are always in relation to others and therefore intersubjective. We can never be truly detached or objective with regard to our situation, others or ourselves. In fact, we cocreate our existence. Bugental (1992) speaks of being 'a-part-of and apart-from', identifying the two ends of the relatedness continuum whilst acknowledging that even at these polarities there is a need for 'the other' to either be with or be apart from. Others can help us fulfil our dreams or can provide obstacles to that fulfilment. Buber, too (1887–1965), devoted much of his thought to the meaning of relatedness, which for him equates to being in dialogue. There are, Buber insists, two basic words, *I-Thou* and *I-It*. One cannot say the word *I* without relating to a world outside the self. These two basic words mark two ways of being in relation to the world. *I-It* relationships are characterised by experiencing, and using objects. These are one-way relationships. The *I* of *I-It* relations understands and experiences the world as one composed of objects locatable in space and time. This way of relating to the world makes no distinction between people and things. It is the domain of determinative causality. These relationships are constituted within the horizon of objective temporality, understood as a network of moments passing from future, to present, to past. *I-Thou* relationships, on the other hand, are two-way relationships based in dialogue. One being encounters another with mutual awareness. *I-Thou* relationships are characterised by 'presentness', and so are also linked to the existential concern of time and temporality, which is reflected in the Jet2 desire to **'Be Present'**.

Let us look briefly at each of Jet2's aspirations from an existential prospective.

Create memories

Jet2 see a relationship between the company and its customers beyond the transactional one of being a temporary component of 'passenger traffic'. It speaks as one human to another who shares the experience of the importance of memories.

Memories also immediately take us to the existential focus on **Time and Temporality**. They are in the moment connections with what has been. Purposely or not, Jet2 is showing an understanding of what it is to be human, including the human desire for **meaning**. We often attempt to make sense of the present by reflecting on the past, looking for resonance or dissonance in the person we are now, have been and will become. Memories are important in the desire for immortality; otherwise, why keep photos and journals? They may have a personal and present meaning, but they also have a future meaning. They may be seen or read by others. They are evidence we existed, and as such they are a little piece of immortality, which will potentially live longer than our bodies will. The choice of what we remember also shows our **values**. Each memory will be meaningful in some way, whether enjoyable or scary. By overtly commenting on memories in its value statement, the company aligns itself to its customers – '...*we make working here a memorable experience for each other too*'. This emphasises the importance given to memories, whether experiencing or mourning the loss of them. In doing so the company immediately provides a human face, connectivity with its customers and staff, and stresses the importance it places on the relational.

In looking to provide a *'swift and safe journey, right down to the little details that mean so much'* Jet2 shows an understanding of the existential desire for **certainty** and safety, and **meaning**. For many people the need to sort out the *'little details'* provides a *sense* of power over uncertainty. If we were to discuss this in a more philosophical context, we would question the reality of that sense of defeating uncertainty, but in the context it is enough to observe that it is a fundamental concept which as humans we have to engage with.

The company's final statement in this section is also relational, *'We're proud to be friendly, approachable, open and honest'*, whilst it also introduces the desire for **authenticity** in the commitment to being *'open and honest'*.

Be present

In this section too, the emphasis is on the **relational**, with concerns expressed equally for the *'nervous customer'* and the *'new colleague'*. The employees are conscious of their **responsibilities** and wish to share power and responsibility with others through empowering and inspiring, *'every colleague is empowered to use their initiative to inspire others'*. The company demonstrates that it knows that it is impossible to do this without respecting others and being truly *'present'* for them.

Work as one team

This section is solely concerned with the relational. Concern is shown for customers and staff, whatever role they hold in the company. The centrality of relatedness is expressed in the statement *'We couldn't do it without our people'*.

Take responsibility

We have seen that **freedom and responsibility** is an important existential consideration. All airlines have the freedom to see their customers primarily as statistics, as income generators or as people. I have no doubt that Jet2 would not offer the service for free and that income generation is vital, but this aim expresses its willingness to take responsibility for its relationship with customers by making their experience as good as possible, in addition to the more concrete responsibilities to be financially prudent, safety conscious and constantly improving.

I have no connection with the company, and cannot know how these aspirations are experienced outside the theoretical framework of a vision statement for the people who work within Jet2. I have flown with them twice, and did find them helpful and personable, thereby embodying their stated values.

Another example of a company that could be considered to be led by shared values is Innocent. As with Jet2, I have no connection with the company and have never visited it or met anyone who works there and, perhaps somewhat surprisingly, have never tried any of its products. I do not know if its practise matches its vision, but I came across the website and decided to use it to check some of my existential concepts and beliefs about what makes an existential vision.

In its vision statement, it declares its purpose as being to,

> 'make natural, delicious and healthy drinks that help people live well and die old...Everything Innocent makes will always be 100% natural, delicious and nutritionally net-positive, so people are physically and mentally better off after they have had our drinks than before. In other words, we want to be a Trojan horse in society, getting as much fruit and vegetables into people as possible, to help us all live well and die old.'

It places emphasis on its values, which are listed as to, 'Be natural, Be entrepreneurial, Be responsible, Be commercial and Be generous'. The page sums up the value-led vision by stating,

> 'When we're all old and grey and sitting in our rocking chairs, we want to be able to look back and be really proud of the business we all helped to create. We think the best way of achieving this is by living the values that are closest to our hearts. Our five values reflect what we are, how we do things, and where we increasingly want to be. And they hang above every loo in the building so we get to remember them everyday'.

They do not leave it there, with just an aspirational statement, but go on to explain how each of the values is embodied in practise.

Be natural

Not just our products, but being natural in how we treat each other and how we speak to everyone – colleagues, drinkers, customers, suppliers, etc. It also means being ourselves, and the best version of it.

Be entrepreneurial

Innocent began as a small, entrepreneurial company, and although we've grown a lot since, we do keep our entrepreneurial mindset. We aren't afraid to do things differently, and we've never given up on a good opportunity.

Be responsible

We keep our promises, are mindful of our impact on our community and our environment, and always try to leave things a little bit better than we found them.

Be commercial

We wouldn't be here if we didn't keep our eyes on the numbers at all times. Ultimately we want to deliver growth for us and our customers too.

Be generous

This means giving honest feedback to one another, helping each other out, taking time to say thank you, and where we can, donating our resources or money to those who need it more than us. It's that simple.'

I believe that these values map easily onto the existential dimensions and core elements, referred to earlier. So, let us first look at the Innocent aims in relation to the four existential dimensions. Innocent seems to address the needs expressed in each dimension – physical, social, spiritual and psychological – in its vision and values. I have mapped them out in Figure 5.1.

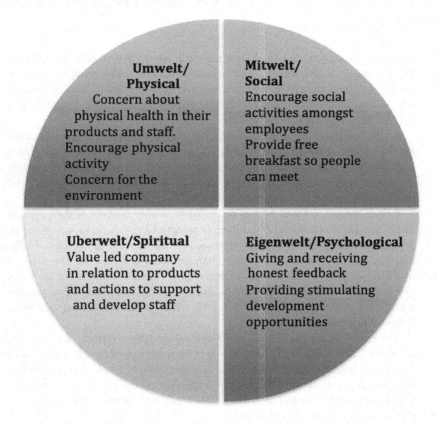

Figure 5.1 Existential dimensions of Innocent business vision.

The core elements

We can undertake the same exercise in relation to core existential elements identified earlier:

Relatedness

We experience ourselves, and everything around us – the world, other people, us included, in the context of a relationship. Innocent gives importance to the company's relationship with its staff, its community and its environment. This reduces existential feelings of being alone. We are fundamentally alone, but Innocent offers a feeling of belonging which somewhat mitigates this for the time we are engaged with the company and beyond.

It remains interested in what people do when they leave Innocent. It is proud of its staff, and celebrates their success, even after they have moved on from their time at Innocent. The website includes some vignettes about what has happened to some past employees. One describes an ex-employee's journey to setting up a Scandi Kitchen:

> *'I became part of the Innocent family back in early 2003 as their first People Team person. In my time at Fruit Towers, I did everything from heading up the People Team to help set up new Innocent offices in new countries to making the original knitting pattern for the Woolly Hats Project. Back then, it was all hands on deck.*
>
> *In 2007, I left to have a baby and to set up my own shop, Scandinavian Kitchen (both of which I decided to do in the same 24 hours). A few years later and the cafe/shop is doing great and we have also expanded to include an online shop and a fancy import-arm to the UK of Scandinavian food products. We work in two locations and we have 11 employees.*
>
> *Before Innocent, I was part of those big blue chip tankers in the City and I couldn't understand why I was forever feeling like something was missing. What Innocent gave me, aside from some of the best years of my life socially, was the freedom and trust to make changes that I believed in. The support and backing from Jon, Rich and Adam to push through radical (at the time) approaches to what "HR" should be like meant that we all together created a fantastic place to work where we would wake up in the morning and think "Wow, I'm going to work today".*
>
> *It is now 4 years since I left and I still refer to Innocent as "we" instead of "them". It is, without a doubt, the best work decision I ever made to leave the money centered job in the big bad investment bank to go work for a place that has grass as carpet. Working in a job that makes you happy – and for people who make you feel motivated, developed and appreciated – is the best gift I ever gave myself work wise.'*

Uncertainty

This related way of experiencing reveals that life, is uncertain. Uncertain in its meaning, uncertain in its future and uncertain because there exists no certainty beyond the finite nature of our existence and the uncertainty itself. No company can address our existential uncertainty. We can never know what will happen today, never mind tomorrow. The company may be very successful one month and losing business the next. However, Innocent shows, with its interest in and celebration of what ex-employees move on to, that there is no hard ending when staff leave. This indicates a collective response to market and life's uncertainties.

Anxiety

This awareness of uncertainty produces an anxiety that is all pervading and never ending. Innocent appears to employ a great deal of transparency in sharing its beliefs, values and ways of working. This reduces staff anxiety. They know what they have joined, they know the company values and whether they match their own, and so existential anxiety is decreased.

Responsibility

The company seems serious about its responsibilities. It does not limit these to its staff and products, but sees its responsibility extending to its community and environment. Furthermore, it shows a commitment to ensuring that its presence on the planet leads to long-term improvement, '*We keep our promises, are mindful of our impact on our community and our environment, and always try to leave things a little bit better than we found them.*'

Meaning

The company offers meaning to its employees in all areas of the four existential dimensions. It is relational within its approach, understanding that we find meaning through our interaction with others. It also understands that people need to get something from working for the company and that this something is not just financial.

> '*Not just our products, but being natural in how we treat each other and how we speak to everyone.*'

Opportunities

The company is not just interested in providing opportunities in the workplace

> '*In a nutshell, our philosophy is that everyone should get something, but the people who contribute the most should get the most: **Salary** – an*

annual pay review ensures that high performance is rewarded by increasing capacity to earn. **Bonus** *– every year if we hit our targets we all get the chance to share in the success.* **Private health care** *– in case you do yourself a mischief at the ping pong table, we have private health care to cover those trips to the physiotherapist.* **Life assurance & critical illness cover** *– we hope nothing bad ever happens to you whilst working at Innocent, but if something was to happen, you're covered with our insurance...We give away three Innocent scholarships every quarter, each worth £1,000, to help a few people do something they've always dreamed of...Each year someone gets an extra week's holiday to work with one of our foundation projects.'*

Evaluate choices

By implication, the company seems to value choice, offering choices between material rewards and learning opportunities and which community projects to fund – *'This means giving honest feedback to one another, helping each other out, taking time to say thank you, and where we can, donating our resources or money to those who need it more than us. It's that simple.'*

Values and beliefs

These are apparent throughout the vision. It starts with the staff the company seeks:

'We want to create a business we can be proud of. So to make this happen, we need brilliant people who inspire and deliver change all around them. That's why we're always looking for talented, ambitious and altruistic folks to come and join us.'

It values these staff and is committed to developing them,

'...So in a business that's growing and evolving like Innocent, the opportunities to develop yourself every day are second to none. That said, we also think it's important to get away from the usual day-to-day stuff, take a step back and improve on the skills you need to be even better at what you do. That's why everyone has regular development chats with their manager to talk about what areas they need to work on to be even better at their job and what their plans for the long game are too...it makes sense for us to have a team of engaged, talented, high performing people at the top of their game. So learning and development is win-win all round.'

Responsibility

The company's commitment to learning and development through to environmental considerations demonstrates its awareness of the breadth of its responsibilities.

'We keep our promises, we are mindful of our impact on our community and our environment, and always try to leave things a little bit better than we found them.'

I doubt that when Innocent drew up its vision it started out with the intention of it being existential. However, I hope I have shown how neatly its vision fits with many of the existential concepts. Given that, how do the values fit into the sale to Coca-Cola? In February 2013, Richard Reed, the founder, denied he was selling out, stating, *'Our aim was to make Innocent a global brand and take its ethical values to the world's consumers. We decided that we would be able to do a better job of that with Coke.'* In a later interview with Emma Featherstone, in *The Guardian* (20.03.17), he pointed out that one of the central values of the company was charitable giving, *'Charitable giving was fundamentally part of the business, it had said it on the packaging for 15 years. That was actually one of the reasons Coke wanted to buy it, the brand message was so strong. Doing a deal with Coca-Cola meant money in to do the things that we've always cared about, which is to get as many healthy products to as many people and places as possible, to build a supply chain that leaves the world a little bit better, and then to give 10% of profits to charity.'* It does seem as though the values have remained intact. Two years after the sale, Dan Germain, who had been with Innocent since the start, reported that there had been *'zero pressure'* from anyone at Coke to change Innocent's model, despite the company running in a *'highly illogical way'*. Those illogical business decisions included giving 10% of its profits to charity – mostly to the Innocent Foundation, which has spent nearly £3 million to date on projects to eradicate hunger. We remain to see what the long-term future holds.

We can choose to develop our organisational vision in an existential way if we so wish. It is a more pertinent approach for twenty-first-century living and thinking. Once we have developed our vision, we need to consider how to communicate it and in business-speak 'get buy-in'. We have already determined that it needs to have clear values and beliefs, which people can share and 'sign up to', and that it needs to address existential givens. If we have succeeded in using that existential approach, how should we go about communicating it?

Communicating the vision: how to take your team with you

Think carefully about how you want to do this. There may be some people who you would like to speak with on an individual basis. Others may form work groups which it would be better to address together. There may also be external partners who need to understand and be inspired by the vision. Whichever way you choose to communicate the vision, McKinsey would suggest you need to consider it in relation to strategy, structure, systems, shared values, style, staff and skills. Existentially, I would consider the place to start is with the shared values and would seek to address all the other aspects through that prism.

One to ones

These will be individual conversations tailored to the needs and concerns of the individual and their individual worldviews, and will call on 'active listening' and 'handling difficult conversations' skills. In communicating a vision and the individual's place within it, we must know that individual well: knowing the values they hold dear, what inspires them and what provides meaning in their work. We should deliver the vision addressing the existential challenges it may present, and the way it fits with, or challenges, the individual's existential needs to address meaning, anxiety and relatedness. If we can do this, the vision is much more likely to appeal to and excite that individual.

Team

Depending on the size of your team and the nature of your organisation, the way you deliver the message will be different. For a large group, you may choose to use a more formal presentation followed by a Questions and Answer (Q&A) session. This may be essential if you are a global company and have to deliver your messages through Skype and conference calls. A smaller group may benefit from a roundtable discussion starting with you outlining the key points and going into detail as questions arise. Just as with the approach described above for speaking with the individual, care needs to be taken to address the existential needs of the group. If working globally, the country's worldview and the nuances of their culture are also important.

External partners

Usually, this will be in the form of a more formal presentation, followed by Q&As. Here is it just as important to align the values driving your vision to the values of your partners. Stakeholders like to see an alignment between their own values and those of a partner organisation. Knowing the worldview of your stakeholders, and indeed, also of your competitors, places you in a stronger position than those companies who ignore the psychological aspects.

Revisiting and deconstructing the vision

Once the vision is sold to others and they have 'bought into it', it can be very tempting to sit back and run with that vision as long as there is no business crisis which demands a rethink. This would be a big mistake. There is a danger that we just run with assumptions and stop reflecting and asking difficult questions. It is important to remember Heidegger and Dru's call for some form of convention-disruption-vision in which we constantly reassess the vision. Leaders need to test their vision against today's reality; disrupt those conventions of thought, belief and behaviour that are no longer meaningful and recreate a new vision which reflects the change in the zeitgeist, the people making up the company and the world outside. Welch (2001) recognised that once the vision is committed to paper, it has not stopped its evolutionary process. The vision will continue to grow and gain shape as the workers interpret and live it. This allows for the vision to be merely the first brush stroke on the canvas which will be jointly created with others. It should not draw a line under creativity, but dare others to try new things within the values and beliefs which are embedded within the framework of the vision, with, as Welch put it, *'the only limits of their creativity and drive'* being *'their own personal standards of excellence'* (in Dobson, Starkey and Richard, 2009, p. 222).

Chapter 6

An existential approach to recruitment, retention and development of staff

Using an existential approach in recruitment

Successful recruiting is vital to every company and organisation, and to every individual seeking a new position. It is important to remember that *'from the existential philosophical perspective, workers are not just blank slates on which management can imprint its instructions. Everything is filtered through the way of thinking of the worker'* (Segal, 2004, p. 45). It is therefore essential that an employer have some understanding of the thinking of a potential worker. Making a wrong choice can be a very painful and expensive experience for everyone concerned.

There are some very obvious transactional procedures which a leader undertakes to help ensure a successful appointment. They are very clear about what competencies and skills are required for the specific post and ensure that these are clearly stated in the papers potential applicants receive. Skills for almost any post will contain a combination of people, thinking, technical and work style skills. Many posts will also require some level of leadership skill. Leaders check that the remuneration offered is commensurate with the level of responsibility and with the technical skills the post calls for and is in line with salaries and benefits of similar posts in the same area of work and geographical context.

Large companies may organise recruitment in house or pay considerable fees to recruitment firms to help with the process. They can produce excellent job descriptions and person specifications, with appropriate salaries and benefits, and present candidates with large amounts of information about the structure of the company and its operations, yet the possibility of making an unsuccessful appointment remains. This is often because more existential considerations are ignored.

Currently, if a large company wants to know the skills and attributes of a potential worker, it turns to specialist external agencies or uses psychometrics to help in the recruitment of staff to managerial and leadership positions. Psychometrics are a set of tests which aim to show the characteristics and skills of applicants by measuring a number of attributes including intelligence, critical reasoning, motivation and personality profile. It could be said that they aim to measure the mind.

It is sometimes considered that an interview process can be fairly subjective and although employers will normally assess skills and experience fairly accurately, much can still be left to gut instinct regarding aligned values. A psychometric test aims to counter subjectivity and provide measurable, objective data aimed at providing a better all-round view of a candidate's suitability. Thus some would argue that psychometric testing offers some 'scientific' credibility and objectivity to the process of recruiting. Traditionally, these tests have taken the form of pen-and-paper or multiple-choice questionnaires, but increasingly they're moving into a digital realm. This means they can be quick and easy to integrate into any stage of the recruitment process.

Tests often attempt to group people into 'types'. Many of the most commonly used, such as Myers-Briggs Type Indicator (MBTI), are based on Carl Jung's archetypal psychological types. Myers-Briggs groups people around the idea of introvert and extrovert personalities, although Jung warned us that there is no such person as a pure introvert or extrovert, suggesting that should such a person exist they would be in a lunatic asylum. However, Myers-Briggs and related tests start from the premise that we have a leaning to introversion or extraversion and that this tendency makes us better suited to some jobs rather than others. In *The Cult of Personality Testing*, Murphy Paul observed that the MBTI has been embraced by numerous lost souls who experience an 'a-ha!' reaction upon learning about their personality type. This can be a little like reading your horoscope and finding that on one particular day it rings true and so assuming that this makes them universally correct.

Enthusiasm for MBTI tests persists despite research showing that as many as three-quarters of people achieve a different personality type when tested again, and the 16 types described by the MBTI have no scientific basis. Murphy Paul (2010, p. 128) argues that *'the MBTI's unfailingly positive tone blends seamlessly with the language of corporate political correctness and with our society's emphasis on promoting self-esteem. The euphemistic blandness of the Myers-Briggs, its mild vocabulary of "fit" and "gift", is the key to its success'*. There is a lot of information out there about the Myers-Briggs preferences and related psychometrics tests, so I am not going to go into these here. Suffice it to say that such tests provide a static assessment of a candidate's personality, and then postulate whether this makes them suitable for a particular post.

There are other popular ways of trying to group people. I am now becoming accustomed to people in the business world introducing themselves to me not just with their MBTI designation, but also identifying themselves as being red, blue or green. Coming from Manchester, I grew up with people introducing themselves as red or blue, but this merely indicated which football team they followed! These business colour designations stem from the growth in the popularity of personality matching through strength deployment inventories, like the one developed by Dr. Elias Porter in 1971, which was based on relational awareness theory. He believed that, *'the more personality theory can **be for** the person rather than **about** the person, the better it will serve the person'*. The colours are ascribed to three different motivational values – the desire to nurture (blue), the desire to be logical/self reliant (green) and the desire to be in action (red). Crudely, these can be considered to equate to being person centred (blue), being analytic (green) and being task centred (red). Each colour has a distinct leadership style associated with it. Blue is linked to leadership based on enablement and support, red on direction and example and green on procedure and exception.

Clearly it is helpful to understand people's motivations. Existentially I would say these are the products of their values and beliefs. Yet, even our values are not static; they change in different contexts. For example, if I were to identify loyalty as one of my values, on first glance it may look like a good value which I can consistently adhere to. However, if I am asked to be loyal to a dictator who requires me to show loyalty through engaging in genocide, or perhaps committing fraud, can I still remain loyal and experience it as a positive value?

It isn't just philosophical issues which perplex us. Unfortunately, psychologists cannot agree among themselves on fundamental issues of personality theory. At least 200 competing definitions are available, and the only theme which can be extracted is that personality is known through the observation of relatively consistent tendencies in people's behaviour. These behavioural tendencies are considered internal powers or traits, exerting control over conduct and so constituting an explanation of it. Tests often measure these personality traits by assessing individuals' answers to questions that purport to assess behavioural themes and by which individuals are compared to others in a group. Particular traits are then reduced to personality factors and are treated as inner causes of behaviour. Such tests cannot measure inner experiences, and, like any tests, they can be prepared for with coaching as to answers most likely to make you the successful candidate for a specific job. This means that it is easy to fake personality tests. Indeed, *The Organization Man* (Whyte, 1956) provides useful instructions for such faking.

The important thing to realise is that one doesn't gain a good score, one merely avoids a bad one. What defines a bad score depends on the impressions of the tester, so even though the use of such tests is promoted as more objective than face-to-face interviews, this may not be the case. According to Whyte, if one wants to get a high score, one should give the most conventional answers possible, admit to liking things the way they are; not worrying much about anything and loving one's parents, partner and children, but not letting them interfere with work. I know that if I were seeking to make an appointment I might be looking for some opposite answers.

Many personality tests use multiple-choice questions. Personally, I struggle with nearly all of these, not just the kind of question where I am asked to choose between a spire and a foundation. I know they are seeking to discover whether I am a practical or an ideas person. However, I am only too well aware that without foundations a spire will collapse. I would need the foundation in order to have the spire. The image of the spire would be more visually appealing than the foundation, but working out what foundations would be needed to hold the spire straight and beautiful would have a different creative excitement and would be an interrelated and vital part of the spire itself. People are complex and able to carry paradoxes. We are wonderfully rich in our capacity to think, so reducing it to a multiple choice can never gain insight into that richness. Of course, it may be considered that for some jobs an employee engaging with that richness may not be what the employer is looking for.

It could seem that multiple-choice seeks to impose or imply certainty – that one answer is right and the others wrong. I usually welcome uncertainty and enjoy the possibility that something we believe to be correct today may be proved to be the opposite later. I once undertook an online course which at the end of each week required students to complete a multiple-choice questionnaire based on the week's required readings. I understood fully that the purpose was to show I had indeed read what had been set and that to 'pass' I merely had to parrot sections of the texts, or just tick the answer which mirrored what was written. I must have driven my tutor mad when each week I failed to do this simple task, which should have been very quick and easy for him to mark. Instead, each week I presented him with short essays as to why I was not making a particular choice of A, B or C. Usually I found myself explaining that although I knew the answer he wanted was B, because it was what had been stated in the text, I could not tick this because I disagreed with the text on that point. I would then follow it by explaining the ways in which I disagreed. I must have been a real pain and yet, authentically, I could not choose to tick something which I believed to be wrong, or over which I would prefer to remain uncertain.

I can only guess at how my behaviour might be interpreted through testing. Perhaps I would be seen as someone who couldn't make decisions, follow instructions or see things through to completion. I think those who know me would argue with those assumptions. In my personal and professional life I am happy making decisions and taking responsibility for the implications of the choice. If I were to be self critical, some of these decisions may be made too quickly, and I may not give others the time they need to think about things. I do have a tendency not to read instructions, often because I believe there is a quicker and more intuitive way to do things. This probably proves right more times than not. When I am wrong it can cause me great problems and prove very time consuming. I can be impatient and I value my time, yet I would prefer to spend quite a long time explaining to a tutor why I was not making a multiple choice, rather than ticking the one I knew they required and quickly moving on. I enjoy completing tasks and rarely start things I don't finish. I believe a short conversation with me would tell people more, and in a more authentic and rich way, about what kind of employee I would make.

So, it is not surprising that not everyone is sold on the success of psychometric testing. Yet, De Cieri and Kramar (2002, p. 96) noted that, '...*the use of personality tests for recruitment purposes in Australian organisations is increasing despite criticism of them as unreliable and unethical.*' They quoted a survey of 8,000 people, in which 44% regarded personality tests as personally invasive. Yet a survey of Australian human resource managers showed that 69% believed personality tests to be valuable tools in improving performance.

Mischel, an Austrian-born American psychologist specialising in personality theory and social psychology, published the controversial book, *Personality, and Assessment*, in 1968, which created a paradigm crisis in personality psychology. The book touched upon the problem in trait assessment that was first identified by Allport (1937). Mischel found that empirical studies often failed to support the fundamental traditional assumption of personality theory that an individual's behaviour, with regard to an inferred trait construct (e.g. conscientiousness; sociability), remained highly consistent across diverse situations. Instead, he cautioned that an individual's behaviour was highly dependent upon situational cues, rather than expressed consistently across diverse situations that differed in meaning. He maintained that behaviour is shaped largely by the exigencies of a given situation and that the notion that individuals act in consistent ways across different situations, reflecting the influence of underlying personality traits, is a myth. The use of personality tests declined following Mischel's findings but soon came back into favour again, although their effectiveness continued to be questioned.

In an article in *Personnel Psychology* in 2007, six respected university professors reconsidered the research on the use of personality testing in work environments. They concluded that faking on self-report personality tests couldn't be avoided, although the important issue is the low validities of personality tests for predicting job performance. Schmitt (2012, p. 95) questioned: *'Why are we looking at personality as a valid predictor of job performance when the validities haven't changed in the past twenty years and are still close to zero?'*

Those of us who are drawn to existential and phenomenological approaches tend to resist labelling, preferring to understand another person not through tests, but through being present to them in order to understand and respond empathically and authentically to their uniqueness. However, it would not be true to say that all existential psychologists are against the use of psychometric testing. Pringle, in her chapter in *Existential Perspectives on Coaching* (van Deurzen & Hanaway, 2012), explains how, within her existential coaching practise, she integrates the use of MBTI assessment, which Pringle describes as being cognition focused, and Fundamental Interpersonal Relations Orientation-Behaviour (FIRO-B), which she describes as being relatedness focused. She uses MBTI tests to help explore and clarify questions such as, 'Who am I? What can I do? How do I differ from others? What are my strengths?' and FIRO-B to show how the client is experienced by others and how this may lead to misunderstandings and conflict. She uses the tests not in a deterministic way, as a definitive assessment tool, but as an aid to further dialogue.

Whatever tools we choose to use in the recruitment process, it is important to establish what makes the candidate the individual they are. Existentially, we would seek to discover the worldview of the candidate, what is important to them (their values and beliefs), what makes something meaningful for them (their spiritual dimension) and where their aspirations lie in terms of increased meaning, as well as financial and status gain. In other words, what makes them tick. As behaviour is linked to our values, we can begin to see how the individual would 'be' and behave within the organisation. This also gives us some basic insight into the coping strategies the person may adopt and what they may prioritise. This approach calls for attentive listening and an intention to be totally present in the selection process. Often interviewers will try to tie candidates down to short answers directly related to a specific question, thus narrowing down the opportunity to gain more insight into the person. Gaining that increased understanding of the person means raising one's head from the matrix of essential and desirable criteria and focusing on the individual. An admirable desire to increase diversity and offer equal opportunity led has to interview processes which require every candidate to be asked exactly the same set of questions and for interviews to last approximately the same amount of time with each person. In many ways this makes good business practise. You will know how long you have to set aside for interviews and be clear what is being asked and in what way. However, there is a danger that much of what makes the candidate special is left undiscovered.

For many years, I held a position in an organisation where I sat on many interview panels. The organisation used clear criteria to make an appointment. Candidates were asked the exactly the same questions and subsequent exploratory questions were not encouraged. This was in the spirit of equality and a desire to avoid managers appointing 'mini mes'. These were admirable objectives, but the process often backfired. The worst appointment I made was of someone so different to myself, and to the majority of the people in the organisation, that it proved very difficult to work collaboratively. It became clear we did not share the same values or work ethic. Whether the fault lay with me, or elsewhere, does not really matter, but it does show one potential problem with trying to be politically correct and working entirely to structures and matrices rather than taking a relational approach.

Probably my best appointment was of my last personal assistant. She was not the highest academically qualified and was interviewed together with a number of very confident and more experienced individuals who looked better on paper and when measured against the job criteria. From the moment she entered the building people were impressed with her attitude, the respect she showed to others, and her interest in them as people. These were important skills for a person-centred organisation which relied on good interpersonal relations with the customers of its services, rather than selling material products. In the interview, her strong values, which were consistent with those of the organisation, were very evident and were her primary motivation in applying for the post. Her skills did not entirely match all the requirements of the assessment matrix but she was clearly the 'best' candidate and we worked together for many years, during which time I facilitated opportunities and financial support for her to pursue the qualifications and training she wished to undertake, so that shortly after I left the company she too left to become the CEO of her own successful business.

Using an existential approach in retaining staff

Retention is another important issue for leaders. Having put considerable thought, time, energy and finances into recruiting a new member of staff, it is important to retain them. It has been estimated that losing a staff member holding a management post costs an organisation up to 100% of their salary. The loss of a senior executive is even more costly.

Yet, many businesses do not give staff retention the priority it deserves. They approach the loss of a valued staff member by taking the attitude 'if they don't want to be here, we don't want them'. This is rather an arrogant and expensive strategy if you consider the potentially high cost of recruitment and induction processes, loss of technical knowledge and skills, additional pressures on other staff whilst the post is vacant, pressure on the recruiting manager, service disruption, lower levels of customer services and satisfaction and the possible loss of business in a climate of uncertainty and low morale.

Some companies try hard to retain staff and conduct carefully thought-out exit interviews to try to discover the specific reasons for people leaving. In theory this is a good idea, but often the person leaving is not comfortable telling a member of the organisation why they are leaving. They usually want to keep things pleasant and just move on. After all, a good reference may be dependent on what they say. Of course, there are other people who will take the opportunity to tell the brutal truth once references are written and a contract for the new job is signed. In my work as an existential coach I often undertake exit interviews for companies and as a neutral outsider, using a phenomenological enquiry approach, discover the heart of a person's decision to leave. This can provide the company with useful insights into organisational and communication structures which are not working for employees, and therefore not for the organisation. The interview may also uncover interpersonal elements such as bullying, harassment and poor management by individuals. The senior leaders must then decide what they choose to do with that knowledge.

People remain with a company for many reasons. Some reasons are pragmatic: salary, retirement and pension plans; flexible working; the length or comfort of the commute from home to office; vacation and other benefits. All are high on the list of reasons why the employees took the job, but they are often not sufficient reason to keep them onboard for the long haul, as it is easy for competitors to match or better these kinds of transactional incentives. For others, there are more existential reasons for staying. They remain with the organisation because it offers them meaning, stimulation, the opportunity to be creative, constructive challenge and the chance to develop themselves. The company and the way in which it treats its staff make them feel respected. For these people it is important that the company have a clear vision with values and beliefs which they share and are happy to 'sign up to', and embodies these in its organisational behaviour and communication. In this way, the organisation makes staff feel 'seen' and 'heard', and valued as a unique and important individual.

Just as there are many reasons for staying, there are equally as many reasons for leaving. Some seem obvious, such as better pay and conditions or increased opportunities for promotion and so on. Yet, people do not always choose to leave for those material reasons. Many causes for people leaving are existential and relational. People leave because they do not get on with others in the company or they dislike the way the company treats them. Often, they have not felt valued or invested in as individuals. Lip service may be given to internal communication but there may be no evidence of it meaning anything or being a catalyst for change. In some ways, those companies who run consultative exercises with the intention of making staff feel they belong and are valued, yet pay little heed to what they learn, are worse than those who make it clear that they are not interested in the thoughts and ideas of their employees. How much worse to use energy in thinking about the company needs, volunteering views and suggestions, only to discover it is all a charade.

Remaining in the company may put a strain on a person's relationship with themselves and their values and beliefs. Even when a person has joined an organisation specifically for the values it holds, they may find that these values are confined to vision and mission statements and not evidenced in the day-to-day behaviour of the people working there, or they may change over time with new leadership or market requirements.

When I consider my own reasons for leaving jobs, they have been related to values, challenges and meaning. I can become bored and need new challenges to help me ward off my boredom. Of course it is not necessarily the work itself or the nature of the company which has become boring, it is just that for me the work has become repetitive and ceased to provide sufficient stimulation. Boredom has a clear relationship with the existential need for meaning. Heidegger has quite a lot to say about boredom (1929/1930 lectures on the fundamental concepts of metaphysics). He links it to a feeling of emptiness (the existential void). The emptiness is of our own making. Another person may not feel emptiness or boredom in the same situation. Heidegger sees this, and I experience it, as an experience of leaving behind my authentic self. The boredom is taking precious moments from our temporal existence and, as Heidegger describes it, it is as though time has come to a halt. In boredom, the significance of the world and the self drain away, motivation ceases and even the temporality of our existence can be altered in a strange way: nothing seems to happen and thus time seems to stand still and seem strangely obtrusive. If the work has become existentially irrelevant, I have a decision to make. I have free will and can choose to use my freedom of choice to escape the void of boredom, to remain in it and feel frustrated or to find a place of acceptance in that boredom. Whichever stance I choose I must then take full responsibility for the choice going forward.

An activity which was once exciting can become boring when we can no longer to see a purpose in it. I need to work in a context which provides me with a meaningful project which will stimulate and challenge me or I become bored and irritated and, no doubt, irritating. Often one is attracted to a post because it seems to offer meaningful stimulation and perhaps initially it does. If you enter a company which has advertised its values as being about promoting positive change, the first year may feel very meaningful as you debate and plan how change can be brought about. However, if no action follows, then planning meetings become boring and depressing wastes of time. Noting the importance of time and temporality in existential thought, the idea of wasting my time and energy on something which no longer has personal meaning and no perceived benefit for others can mean that the work has become meaningless. Positive change is an imperative for the true existentialist; otherwise, existence is a complete void. To put it another way, it is not always simply enough to 'be'. One has to be 'something' or life truly lacks meaning or purpose. From this point of view, existentialism has the potential to be a very positive means of approaching reality. Nothing in existential thought dictates a negative view of humanity or reality. In fact, much of the philosophy revolves around the limitless capacity for ethically and intellectually engaged persons to enact change in the world.

To provide meaning for a member of staff requires clearly articulated ethics and values, with the ethos and behaviour of the organisation matching these aspirational and publically stated values and desires. It is painful to find oneself in a post which does not match up to the stated values which attracted one to the company in the first place.

Business literature is not short on practical suggestions of how to retain staff. Much of it focuses on the need to ensure that financial and benefits packages are attractive and remain so within the competitive market. Of course this is important, and may be central in the worldview of some employees. However, this is not necessarily the case for all. As outlined above, some people will place more importance on the meaning, stimulation and the satisfaction they take from their work. It is paramount to some people that work is a place where they can authentically pursue their quest for meaning.

Whatever a person's values, be they primarily monetary or ethical, the desire for communication and relatedness is always present. People need to know what is expected of them, how much freedom they have or do not have and how well they are perceived to be doing their jobs. Humans seek meaning, relationship and recognition. We are all conscious of our need to maintain our self-esteem, to feel we have a place and to be respected for ourselves and what we bring to the workplace. Our search for meaning can lead to us wanting to feel part of something bigger than ourselves, which aligns with our values.

People need to feel heard, seen and valued for the uniqueness of their existence. Each person may require different things in order to feel appreciated and respected. This can be an important element in retaining staff. Some companies chose to recognise the value of their staff through reward *systems*. However, what some people experience positively, others may experience more negatively. For many years if I received praise for something which I did not feel I had done particularly well, I experienced this as condescending, and questioned the judgement and authenticity of those giving the praise. One of my daughters must have picked up similar values. One day I found the wastebasket in her bedroom full of 'merit certificates' which gave points for good behaviour or high-quality work. When I asked her why they were in the bin, she explained that the idea was that when you received 10 certificates, the head teacher would exchange them for a gift token. She felt the system was unfair as she received several certificates each week without working particularly hard, whereas she saw others, who in her opinion tried harder, not being rewarded. The unfairness, together with the embarrassment of being seen regularly going to the head teacher's office and receiving vouchers, made the whole reward scheme unpleasant for her.

Any organisational reward or recognition scheme needs to match the values of the organisation and those working in it, or it can misfire badly. I worked with one organisation which had a very strong identity. The founder wanted it to be an inclusive, stimulating and enjoyable place to work, with the staff experiencing it as an alternative family. Unfortunately, he only considered what would make a work environment attractive to him. He chose to set up in a beautiful building in the middle of the countryside, with fabulous views. He then kitted it out a little like Willy Wonka's sweet factory with dispensing machines containing all kinds of brightly coloured, sugary sweets attached to the walls in each room, which staff could access throughout the day. On Fridays he would personally organise a BBQ, buying the food and drink and cooking it himself. He had a blanket rule that no one was to wear shirts and ties. It was his perfect working environment but did not necessarily fit with the worldview of his staff or the needs of the business. Several of the people working there were vegetarians and hated having slabs of meat carried in for the Friday BBQ. They did not want to attend but felt that they would be considered 'outcasts' if they didn't. Others enjoyed the food, but at times needed to give attention to tight work deadlines at that time rather than attend. They felt trapped, believing that if they did not attend they would 'be in trouble' and the same would be true if they failed to make their work deadlines. The ban on shirts and ties also created problems. Most of the staff were very happy that it was fine to wear shorts and flip flops in hot weather, but would have preferred it to be a choice and felt that they lost business when visiting clients were told not to come wearing suits. The remote location was also a problem for staff and customers, particularly in bad weather. The general feel was that their customers were not shown respect by the organisation's insistence that they dress and act in a particular way. They took this as evidence that their own individuality would not be respected and instead of creating the relaxed environment he had wanted, he had created a very tense team. Lyons, in his book *Lab Rats* (2019), describes similar experiences when working for Hubspot, with its beanbag chairs, table tennis tables and fridges stacked with beer. He welcomed the flexibility, the free snacks and the hammock in which staff could take a nap, but what he had been seeking most was job security. He came to understand that this fast-growing start-up offered even less job security than any of the failing magazines where he had previously worked. What makes us happy in our work differs from individual to individual and can be polar opposites. Some people thrive on being busy, working to tight deadlines and embrace uncertainty and change, whilst others seek routine, certainty and relaxation. We must learn what is important to individual people through listening to them, engaging in dialogue and clear, clean communication.

I doubt many people would argue with the belief that feeling respected and being part of something which has meaning requires excellent communication. Such communication is not one-way and so in addition to clear expression it requires listening and attending to others. However, we cannot assume that because we have said something it has been heard and understood, or that we always understand what is being said to us. We are often too quick to jump to the assumption of understanding without checking that it is correct. We need to feedback and summarise what we have heard and be open to being corrected when we have it wrong in order to guard against misunderstandings. This is particularly true with new staff members who may not have picked up the nuances of the communication styles of the organisation or their new colleagues, and may also feel embarrassed about admitting that they are not understanding what is being said to them.

Even if we get the words right and check that we have been understood, this may still not be enough. Communication is not just about the words but equally about the level and quality of attention given to the person being addressed. This can be expressed through the tone of voice, combined with eye contact, hand gestures, body positioning and even touch. We all occasionally need that proverbial 'pat on the back'. Dr Edward Wertheim of Northeastern University D'Amore-McKim School of Business found that a large percentage of the meaning we derive from communication (over 90%) is derived from nonverbal cues. So, if you rarely meet face to face with your team, relying instead on 'virtual communication' or communication cascaded down through a hierarchy of management, much can be 'lost in translation'. Not only is there a danger of miscommunication, but also if communication is sparse or inadequate, an employee can feel isolated and confused and may seek to address this by a move to another company.

Good communication is the start of empowerment. If people are clear about the boundaries of their responsibilities and freedoms, then they can 'play' creatively, taking ownership and pride in their work. Employees who feel stifled in their desire for innovation will move on very quickly. Those who feel scared to try new things because they fear criticism or blame will become frustrated. If people receive no feedback, then they can feel lost, undervalued and demotivated. These are all classic reasons for leaving a company.

As a leader, people will look to learn from you. You should equally look to learn from them, as we all bring our unique experiences and interpretations to the table. By being a flexible and accessible leader who encourages creative thinking and who takes an authentic interest in the ideas and critiques of others, people will feel engaged and valued, and show more commitment to the organisation. On the whole, people do not just need to have their strengths acknowledged, they wish to build on them through the availability of regular honest feedback and the availability of development opportunities. Such opportunities provide a strong incentive for ambitious and talented team members to stay in the company and use their learning for the benefit of the organisation. Unless employees can try new opportunities, take on challenging tasks and attend meaningful training opportunities, they will stagnate. Some people respond well to individual coaching, whereas others benefit more from group experiences. An existential leader will know their team well enough to offer appropriate opportunities and encourage self-awareness and self-questioning.

I have noted that work may be a place for people to address existential loneliness and to develop a sense of belonging. Of course, the opposite can also be true, with an individual feeling more isolated and abandoned. The existential leader will be aware of the importance of addressing this, whilst holding on to the truth that we are all different, and so require different things in order to feel we belong. Generally when people work together, they can achieve more than they would have individually. Yet, this is only true when there is a culture of collaboration that accommodates individuals' working styles and talents. There is something of a cult of team working at present, and when people are seeking a new post they are likely to encounter interview questions aimed at finding out how good a team player they are. Although this is important, it is vital not to overlook what an individualist can bring to the organisation.

The first experience of belonging, relatedness or isolation will take place in the early days of starting a new post. However, induction, 'on boarding' and orientation are often not given much thought. Often, in higher-level posts it does not happen at all. It may be assumed that the level of experience which helped gain the candidate a post means that there is nothing left for them to learn. This is far from the case. A person entering a company at the leadership level is likely to have worked elsewhere for a number of years and will have picked up, or even created, the ethos and behaviours of their previous organisation, which may be very different from the one they are joining. Whatever the level of post, from day one a leader will start to create a real relationship with the new staff member, ensuring that the company culture is clear and encouraging the newcomer to be actively engaged in developing that further through discussion and debate.

Periods of transition can be made easier through *mentorship programmes* in which a new employee is paired with an experienced mentor from whom they can learn the ropes. A good mentor will also use the fresh eyes of the new employee to see how the company appears to them and to learn from their fresh perspective. Mentors shouldn't be work supervisors, but they can offer guidance and be a sounding board for newcomers, welcoming them into the company culture.

When we explored the existential dimensions, we considered the need for some balance across them. People need a balanced existence, attending to all dimensions, even if only to acknowledge that one is less important to them than others. The need for work-life balance is important in staff retention and an existential leader will show that they understand this. Many employees are just as concerned about the quality of life as they are about the amount of money a position offers. Some companies are very aware of the physical environment on offer in and around their business, and provide opportunities for employees to benefit from these. Understanding that people have a life outside work can be evidenced through offering flexible hours and work-at-home options. Some companies address other needs by allowing employees to bring a pet to work or to power-nap during the day. If a person's needs are being attended to, they are more likely to stay.

Earlier, I have written about the importance of relatedness to existential thought, and mentioned it in the context of many of the leadership challenges. It is equally, if not more, important in the context of retaining staff. Sartre's famous quote 'Hell is other people' (from his 1943 French play *No Exit* [*Huis Clos*]) speaks of the experience of being trapped in a deadlock with other people. He claims there is no need for 'red-hot pokers' to make us feel bad, as it is the presence of other people which make it hell. For Sartre, shame is the original feeling brought on by the realisation of the existence of others. The moment one sees oneself as other people may see you, that is, as an object, brings shame. For Sartre it is the crushing realisation that one is little more to others than the physical manifestation of the body in their sight. In this situation we feel the power of the Other, the power to freeze us into a being that we are not. The gaze of others exposes us, makes us weak and fragile and turns us into objects. In work, we can see others as a help or as a hindrance in reaching our goals. Whichever way we see it, those around us are vital in how we experience things. It is natural to judge ourselves against others and to be sensitive to how they perceive us and the assumptions that leads to. Leading existentially makes one sensitive to these vulnerabilities in others and in ourselves. People leave companies more often because of poor relationships with colleagues, managers and supervisors than because of their job. Providing high-quality, supportive, encouraging and stretching management and supervision makes retention more likely. Knowing that conflicts will occur means that an existential leader will develop structures to minimise the damage that conflict may cause through actively taking measures to prevent, manage and resolve conflict. I have devoted a later chapter to how this may be done.

Authenticity is also important in providing a sense of security, which can be a reason for remaining in a company. We know that nothing in life is certain, but if we can trust that all challenges will be met in a truthful way and believe that we are respected and cared for within that context, then we can be more secure in our understanding. If change is to occur, even if it is to bring negative consequences for an individual, it is important, as a leader, to be truthful and engage openly with the possibilities which are open and those which are not. People usually are aware when negative news is coming, and trying to protect them from it adds to their anxiety. If they know what is happening, or likely to happen, they can plan accordingly and take responsibility for their own reaction and their own future.

Many companies buy in Employee Assistance Programmes (EAPs) in the hope that they can support staff with mental health, depression, disillusionment and possibly some of the existential issues I have highlighted. These programmes usually offer between 4–6 sessions of cognitive behavioural therapy (CBT). Recently the usefulness of CBT has been questioned, and Dalal (2018) sees the use of CBT as tied into old-style leadership and management practises, far removed from the search for meaning outlined above. He considers that CBT psychology has fetishised measuring to such a degree that only what is countable is considered to be of importance. He goes so far as to suggest that CBT it is not just 'bad' science but 'corrupt science', fostered by neoliberalism and the phenomenon of New Public Management, with its core of managerialist mentality and its hyper-rational understanding of 'efficiency', both of which are commonplace in organisational life today. He considers CBT an exercise in symptom reduction, vastly exaggerating the degree to which symptoms are reduced and the durability of the improvement, as well as the numbers of people helped. This is a contentious issue in the land of therapy and not for discussion here, but I don't think there is any argument that CBT, and the most prevalent workplace counselling-based support which leaders offer, mainly ignores the more complex philosophical and existential ailments which people may be battling. I do not work for EAPs or offer CBT, but I do supervise many counsellors and therapists who do. Some get great satisfaction from enabling people to reduce their symptoms enough to return to the workplace, whilst others feel frustrated that they cannot address the real, more philosophical challenges their client is facing, fearing that they have merely done enough to get them back to work where the problem is likely to resurface. Some leadership models would agree that the leader's responsible is solely to get, and keep, someone in the workplace, whilst others would recognise a broader responsibility. I would suggest that making work more existentially meaningful could reduce some of the need for current support models.

Using an existential approach in the development of staff (including an introduction to existential coaching and mediation)

Leaders recognise that their most important resource is the people in their organisation. It is imperative that we care for, respect, encourage and develop this resource. Our success as leaders and the success of our organisations are dependent on their work, requiring us to commit to both developing ourselves as leaders and to developing our staff.

Day (2001) provides an exploration of leadership development from three interrelated perspectives: theory, practise and research. He differentiates between 'leader development' and 'leadership development'. He sees the first as focused on the individual leader – what leaders are and do – whilst the second is focused on the wider picture, taking in organisational dynamics and context. His research found little evidence of success in the programmes he looked at, but he identified six influential techniques for leadership development – 360° feedback, coaching, mentoring, networking, job assignments and action learning. These 'techniques', or approaches, as I would prefer, can be existential in flavour and beneficial in leader development, leadership development and the development of staff at all levels.

We develop staff in many ways, including targeted training for individuals and teams, and mentoring and coaching for individuals. Training and staff development has always been a feature of organisational behaviour, even sometimes if only in its absence. Kostenbaum and Block (2001) appear to question how well the perceived responsibility of leaders to develop their staff fits with an existential approach. I have already drawn attention to the importance of freedom in existential beliefs and values, so, the question is: If we accept that each employee has freedom and accountability, can we still, from an existential viewpoint, hold that it is the responsibility of the organisation to develop those people working in it? Kostenbaum and Block suggest that to take on this responsibility may equate to a position of the organisation 'owning' or 'possessing' 'its people'. They suggest that if we move away from this, and place the responsibility and freedom onto the individual, allowing them to choose their own way of learning, define their own learning goals and figure out how and when to pursue them, it breaks with the established understanding that any employee who exceeds management expectations will be taken care of favourably. This does not lead to a belief that development and training is not important, but contains a call for it to be more participative from the beginning when learning goals are identified and the nature of the training planned. Ideally this happens in regular one to ones and, more formally, in a jointly owned appraisal process.

One role of leadership is to identify and offer a range of development opportunities. Over the years there has been rapid change in the nature and style of such training courses for managers and leaders. Lyons (2019) blames some of these well-intentioned and innovative training initiatives for some of the unhappiness with work which he found in his research. He describes his own experience of Lego Serious Play (LSP), which has been used since 2010 as a way of fostering creative thinking. Participants work through imaginary scenarios using visual three-dimensional Lego constructions, hence the name 'serious play'. The experience did not sit well with Lyons, who claimed that instead of making people happier, 'silly, touchy-feely workshops' aimed at self-improvement and transformation resulted in increased unhappiness. Some individuals use metaphors constantly in their thoughts and language and would welcome the potential for the creativity which LSP may present. However, Lyons experienced the exercise of having to build a duck from Lego as extremely stressful. He considered that for many people, especially those over 50, it compounded a fear that they were out of place or past their sell-by date and so may shortly be out of a job. I question the universality of this statement, particularly in relation to the age factor, but agree that this type of training can feel very exposing, and may often be experienced as a threat to self-esteem. We can feel judged and therefore vulnerable. Lyons goes on to say that the younger workers he spoke with also disliked this type of training, likening it to joining a cult where one had to do whatever you were told, no matter how ridiculous it may seem. The aim of increasing creativity may have the opposite effect if a participant has a brilliant new idea which they feel would be better expressed in plasticine rather than Lego! Instead of widening the boundaries of possibility, it may inadvertently restrict them. I am not advocating that training should be restricted to the comfort zone of the participant. Indeed, in the first term of a Fine Art degree I learned that amongst other things I was required to learn arc welding. My first thought was, 'hey, I'm a painter, why do I need to do that?', quickly followed by the acknowledgment to myself that the thought of wearing a heavy metal helmet that would pitch me into total darkness was terrifying. It was explained to me that if I knew I was capable of arc welding, then if the day ever came when I suddenly had a wonderful idea for a sculpture requiring that skill, I would not abandon that idea through fear. Even today I am still awaiting that idea! However, the rationale did make sense to me, and I felt a certain satisfaction in wearing the helmet and successfully completing a tiny piece of welding.

Trends in the styles of training programmes come and go. Existentially based training aims to provide a philosophical and psychological framework based on the existential givens we all share, and therefore carries an increased possibility of being meaningful across time, age, gender, race and culture. Despite growing interest in the role of the existential approach in business, there are still very few business training programmes which overtly take an existential stance.

Where they do exist, Existential Leadership programmes consider a number of aspects of leadership. These include how the leader may.

- Remain authentic.
- Find their role and that of the organisation meaningful.
- Understand the importance of relationships and develop the skills to create and maintain them.
- Consider organisational values, beliefs and behaviours in a holistic way.
- Acknowledge that each of us exists in a number of existential dimensions.
- Make meaningful choices and decisions based on a understanding of freedom, responsibility and consequences for self and others.
- Plan within an acceptance of time and temporality and the impossibility of certainty.

All these aspects are continually in play in the leadership role, including in the strategic and financial arenas. It is hard to see how they can still be ignored in so much of current leadership training.

Given the rarity of existential leadership training programmes there is always the capacity for taking an existential approach when choosing the development opportunities on offer or devising new ones. Essentially, to be existentially informed, they must be meaningful to the individual engaging in them, as well as to the organisation, and the content needs to be in line with individual values and beliefs, or if they are not, then there must be the opportunity for authentic and open challenge rather than blind adherence. We know that different people have different worldviews, including language preferences, some preferring straight-talking, factual language whilst others are more at home with the use of narrative and metaphor. The manner in which training is delivered will suit one individual more than another, and individuals are likely to get more from the training if it is offered in a language style they can engage with. Participants need to feel they can personally evaluate the relevance of the training and honestly feed back their views to the organisation.

If an organisation provides training or workshops to examine the ethos of the organisation, something that often happens when companies are considering their vision and strategic plans, it is vital that the company 'practise what it preaches'. I have experienced development initiatives which were so clearly inauthentic that they were amusing. On one occasion the board of an organisation decided without any prediscussion with leaders and managers that it wished to move from a transactional leadership model to a transformational one. All senior leaders received an email **instructing** them that they **must** attend 'transformational' training on a certain date. This instruction was so far removed from the spirit of a transformational approach that, although amusing, it cast serious doubt on the authenticity of their desire to change anything. They chose a very directive communication to imply they were moving away from a directive leadership style!

Finding an authentic training programme which fits individual and organisational needs and values can be quite a difficult task. It may be easier to create a more individualised development plan with participants choosing training programmes which they identify as relevant to themselves and useful to the organisation, developing the contents of a new programme based on collaboration between trainers and potential participants or through offering one-to-one mentoring or coaching. As a leadership trainer I relish the opportunities to meet early in the process with the leaders who may be attending the training, to identify with them what their priorities are, to discuss any fears or ambivalences they may hold towards particular training methods (e.g. the use of roles, which often creates panic in the thoughts of potential participants) and the correlation or difference between what they individually want from the training and what they believe to be organisational requirements. Once we have clarified these things we can acknowledge that no training will cover everything sufficiently for each individual but that training is a joint endeavour where trainer and participant will take responsibility for trying to address as many of those needs as possible within the contextual constraints and focus of the training. This approach seeks to embed the existential requirements for authenticity, freedom and responsibility and relatedness.

Training programmes are usually group activities yet some people respond better to a one-to-one approach. This is often offered as coaching or mentoring. Mentoring is often seen as a form of coaching, and indeed, much of what follows has relevance to both coaching and mentoring. I have worked as both a mentor within an organisation I worked in and as an external coach. I want to briefly state what I see as the differences. *Mentoring* is most often defined as a professional relationship in which an experienced person, the *mentor*, assists another, the mentee, in developing specific skills and knowledge that will enhance the less experienced person's professional and personal growth within the context of their current work. The implication here is that the mentor holds specific skills and experience in the type of work the mentee is engaged in and often works, or has worked, in the same company.

In a 'Thought Paper' produced by Management Mentors, an American company, in 2013, the authors identify 25 ways in which they see coaching and mentoring differing. I do not agree entirely with their findings. In many of their examples I would consider the reverse to be true. They define the overall difference by saying that *'Coaching is about skills and knowledge acquisition. Mentoring is transformational and involves much more than simply acquiring a specific skill or knowledge'*. This does not fit well with my understanding and practise of existential coaching, which is not focused on skill and knowledge acquisition, but on a philosophical exploration of the presenting dilemma, thus making it essentially transformational. They also see mentoring as being *'about a relationship and involves both the professional and the personal'*, going on to liken it to counselling. For an existential coach, relational aspects of the clients' being-in-the-world, and more specifically of their 'being-in-the-workplace', lie at the heart of the coaching and the client is not seen solely within the professional dimension, although that is where the work will focus.

Management Mentors offers a chart of the perceived differences between mentoring and coaching. This is shown in columns 1 and 2. In column 3, I offer my thoughts on how these areas fit with my view of existential leadership coaching practise (Table 6.1).

As we can see, as with so many things, there is no consistent universal agreement about what is mentoring and what is coaching. Does this really matter? I would suggest that what is needed is for the coach/mentor and the client/coachee to explore what is needed by the client and the organisation, and what is possible and what is not. This would include being clear about levels of expertise (interpersonal and technical); professional boundaries, including 'ownership of the work', whether the focus is primarily with the client or the organisation and the subsequent confidentiality limitations and report-back methods which will flow from that clarity. In the following sections I shall refer throughout to coaching, not mentoring. It is for you to decide how much of what follows relates to both.

For some leaders, coaching may feel a step too far, a little 'touch feely', holding therapeutic connotations which may not at first sit comfortably in a business context. However, Western (2013), in his critical text on leadership, discusses what he termed 'the therapist leader discourse' with its focus on subjectivity and identity at work, drawing attention to Nelson's book *Make More Money by Making Your Employees Happy* (2012), in which he asserts that happier employees are more productive and therefore make more money for the company. Over the last 15 years there has been a profound change in how coaching is viewed. In the past it was often seen as remedial, implying it was needed because there was a business problem, or an individual was failing in some way. This stigma and negativity has declined, so that coaching now can be perceived as affording status: coaching has become an indication that one's company considers one worth an investment.

Table 6.1 Monica Hanaway (2019) in response to 'Coaching vs. Mentoring: 25 Ways They're Different. A Thought Paper for Sharing', Management Mentors (2013)

Coaching (as defined by management mentors)	Mentoring (as defined by management mentors)	Existential leadership coaching
Task oriented	Relationship oriented	Value led, meaning oriented, but will consider task and relationship.
Short term	Long term	Short-term contracts which can be extended.
Performance driven	Development driven	Development driven based on increased personal insight.
Can be done as needed; no design necessary	Program design needed to create effective program	No preprepared programme designed. Focus is cocreated and reviewed during the process.
Manager directly involved	Manager involved only indirectly	Manager or client may commission the work, after which the manager is usually not involved.
More easily evaluated and measured by ROI	Less easy to measure for ROI	Less easy to measure for ROI. The client is the main assessor of the success of the coaching.
Reliance on performance management systems, e.g. reviews, 360s etc.	Not dependent upon performance management systems	Not dependent upon performance management systems. Any measurement criteria would be agreed upon by coach and client and based on increased personal insight, more confident decision-making and analysis of consequences (freedom and responsibility).
Feedback by coach to manager about progress in development	No feedback from mentor to manager	An existential coach would maintain confidentiality and not report back unless this was agreed to in advance. Sometimes the coaching identifies organisational issues which need addressing and these would be feed back to a person designated by the leader. However, most leaders choose to do this themselves rather than expect the coach to do so.
Coach paid for services	Mentor receives no compensation	Existential coach is paid for services.

(Continued)

Table 6.1 (Continued) Monica Hanaway (2019) in response to 'Coaching vs. Mentoring: 25 Ways They're Different. A Thought Paper for Sharing', Management Mentors (2013)

Coaching (as defined by management mentors)	Mentoring (as defined by management mentors)	Existential leadership coaching
Coach operates independently	Mentors operate with assistance from the mentoring programme manager	Existential coach operates independently.
No training of coachee needed	Mentors and mentees trained	The existential coach is looking for an authentic relationship and dialogue with the client which any training or detailed preparation may inhibit. The coach will explain any ground rules, boundaries or other limitations at the start.
Focus is more on business issues than personal	Focus is on the personal and professional development	In existential leadership coaching in a business setting, the starting point is the professional. However, the 'being'/personal aspects play a large part in business decisions and behaviours and will be explored within the context of the existential dimensions with an emphasis on exploring implications for the client's leadership role.
Lower initial investment cost	Higher initial investment cost	Lower initial investment cost
Lends itself to online software	Management of the mentoring program lends itself to software but not the relationship itself	Does not lend itself to online software as it is a relational embodied approach.
Coaches leave organisation when done	Mentors and mentees remain in the organisation and can provide ongoing mentoring to others	Existential coaches usually leave the organisation when done. However, the freshness of the approach can mean that the organisation wants a permanent change of ethos as a result. This may result in the coach being invited to take on another role working with a broader group of people within the organisation.

(Continued)

Table 6.1 (Continued) Monica Hanaway (2019) in response to 'Coaching vs. Mentoring: 25 Ways They're Different. A Thought Paper for Sharing', Management Mentors (2013)

Coaching (as defined by management mentors)	Mentoring (as defined by management mentors)	Existential leadership coaching
Done by inside or outside content expert	Mentors are normally within the company	Existential coaches are neutral and outside the organisation. They may hold the sessions in the organisational venue or elsewhere.
Can be done for remedial purposes	Never remedial	Not remedial.
Internal politics not usually affected	Internal politics a consideration in program design	In any leadership coaching, internal politics are likely to have a significant part to play in the client's dilemmas and the implications of any changes resulting from the coaching.
Cultural change may/may not occur	Mentoring is transformational and affects culture	Existential coaching is transformational and is likely to affect culture.
Coaching done 1-on-1	Mentoring most often done 1-on-1, but other models may be used as well	Existential coaching usually 1-on-1 but may include group coaching.
Diversity may or may not be included	Diversity is a component of mentoring	Diversity and a person's relationship with it are part of the relational aspect.
Content expertise more important in coaching	Interpersonal skills more important in mentoring	Relational aspects are at the heart. The emerges from the dialogue, although their may be an agreed-upon starting point/presenting problem.
Manager may be coach of own employee	Mentor is outside the mentoree's direct supervisory line	Neutrality and independence are important in existential leadership. An existential leader may use existential coaching skills with an employee but would not be their 'coach'.

(Continued)

Table 6.1 (Continued) Monica Hanaway (2019) in response to 'Coaching vs. Mentoring: 25 Ways They're Different. A Thought Paper for Sharing', Management Mentors (2013)

Coaching (as defined by management mentors)	Mentoring (as defined by management mentors)	Existential leadership coaching
Coaching is one directional	Mentoring is bidirectional	As existential leadership coach works across all the existential dimensions and concerns. It is multidirectional in content. In terms of who gains from the coaching relationship, the coach is focused on the needs of the client. However, as with any encounter with a fellow human being, we learn something. For the existential coach this is a by-product of the work, which the coach would reflect on and take ownership of to use for their own self-development. It is important for all coaches to recognise what is 'their stuff' and what is the client's.
Coaching is focused on the business person	Mentoring involves the whole person	Existential leadership coaching is focused on the business dilemmas brought to the coaching, but also engages with the client holistically, regarding their business role as part of their being-in-the-world-with-others. If they are a different person in business than elsewhere, they are not living authentically. This does not exclude the possibility that they may choose to behave in a way fitting with the context, whilst at the same time remaining consistent to their values and beliefs.
Behavioural transformation	Personal transformation	Gains in personal insight and transformation are usually reflected in behavioural change. If this were not the case it could be seen as living in 'bad faith'.

This change is not just a change in business culture itself, but reflects that, on the whole, people are wanting more from work. People are taking a more holistic view of their working life and looking to their workplace to find answers to some existential questions. This makes it more likely that they are willing to admit to themselves, and to others, that they need the help of professionals to understand themselves and to grow and develop in their working environment. Senior executives are more willing to acknowledge they use coaching and that it has informed them as leaders and influenced their value systems, the way they deal with other people or their approach to their work. This is increasingly seen as something to be proud of and evidence of emotional intelligence and insight.

Leaders may choose to avail themselves of the services of a coach. They may also choose to bring a coaching approach to their leadership style, using the approach themselves with some members of their team.

Coaches are individuals and will have their own coaching styles and methodology. In this chapter I am focusing on staff development through the use of an existential coaching approach. The philosophical underpinnings of this approach are transferable to mentoring and training programmes. The approach may be integrated into a transformative leadership model or provided through external existential coaches, although these are still relatively thin on the ground.

Existential coaching uses the philosophical framework introduced earlier, drawing on the work of Heidegger, Sartre, Kierkegaard and others to underpin its approach. It works with the same issues as other coaching approaches, but an existential coach may focus particularly on existential issues such as freedom, responsibility, authenticity, purpose, meaning, paradox and dilemma. All these existential concerns are to be found at the heart of the myriad reasons that cause people to seek coaching, specifically leadership coaching.

Like other existential therapeutic approaches, existential coaching employs the phenomenological method of enquiry. I shall just recap quickly what I mean by this. In recent philosophy of mind, the term 'phenomenology' is often restricted to the characterisation of sensory qualities of seeing, hearing and so on: that is, what it is like to have sensations of various kinds. However, our experience is normally much richer in content than mere sensation. Accordingly, in the phenomenological tradition, phenomenology is given a much wider range, addressing the meaning things have in our experience, notably, the significance of objects, events, tools, the flow of time, the self and others, as these things arise and are experienced by the individual in the 'now' of our 'life-world'.

Phenomenology can be seen as studying the structure of various types of experience ranging from perception, thought, memory, imagination, emotion, desire and volition to bodily awareness, embodied action and social activity, including linguistic activity. The structure of these forms of experience typically involves what Husserl called 'intentionality', that is, the directedness of experience toward things in the world, the property of consciousness that it is a consciousness of, or about, something. According to classical Husserlian phenomenology, our experience is directed toward, that is, it represents or 'intends' things only through particular concepts, thoughts, ideas, images and so on. These make up the meaning or content of a given experience, and are distinct from the things they present or mean.

Furthermore, in a different dimension, we find various grounds or enabling conditions, the conditions of the possibility or intentionality, including embodiment, bodily skills, cultural context, language and other social practises, social background and contextual aspects of intentional activities.

A coaching approach grounded in these existential and phenomenological concepts provides an opportunity for a leader to explore their relationship to all these dimensions and to consider leadership dilemmas through the prism of this philosophical approach.

What is the aim of existential coaching?

Existential coaching shares the general aims of other coaching models. Coaching was initially developed in the areas of sport and education. It gained momentum in the 1980s with the publication of Gallwey's *The Inner Game* in 1986. Gallwey, a tennis coach, extended the breadth of coaching to include not just the practical but the psychological, considering that the opponent in one's head was a greater challenge than the opponent on the other side of the net. Whitmore (1992), who developed the influential GROW model as a structure for the coaching, also came from a sporting background, being a former motor racing champion. By the 2000s, coaches were calling for an increased repertoire of techniques, considering that the sports-based approach worked well in developing behavioural and presentation skills, but did not work so well in developing assertiveness or influencing skills as it failed to pay sufficient attention to underlying personal issues, emotions, anxieties and personal traits. This led Garvey (2008) and others to call for a more sophisticated model drawing on psychotherapy and organisation consulting, with a foundation based on a respect for ethics and boundaries.

Just as with other coaching approaches, existential coaching aims to facilitate the development of an increased understanding and new perspective on the way we live, to increase the client's awareness of themselves, the world in which they exist and the future that they want. Through increased understanding of their worldview, it becomes possible to ask new authentic questions about life.

It is not a solution-driven approach, and existential coaches will express caution in providing solutions. It suggests answers come more profoundly, and potentially more beneficially, by staying still and paying attention to what is in front of you rather than attempting to fix or direct it. By not directing or leading the client, there is an increased likelihood that any outcomes will be personally meaningful to the client and so more likely to be acted upon.

The starting point for the approach is philosophical, yet although there is room for philosophical debate and contemplation in a coaching relationship; ultimately it is, *'an approach with an entirely pragmatic objective: to help people to live their lives with greater deliberation, liberty, understanding and passion'*. (van Deurzen & Hanaway 2012, p. xvi). So, don't let the idea that it is essentially philosophical put you off. Existential coaching works with everyday issues in both our professional and personal lives.

At the heart of the approach is the belief that we are all individuals, and yet as humans, we share some core 'givens' which we cannot escape. We are all born alone and we shall die alone and the journey between those two points will be paved with anxiety and a search to give meaning to our temporal state. We may seek companionship in this journey and so benefit from having a coaching relationship which facilitates our exploration of our own being and of the dilemmas and challenges that will inevitably be thrown up for us as we travel our unique path. This is particularly true for leaders, whose position is often quite a lonely one.

The skills and approach in coaching from an existential perspective are framed around the same existential concerns and dimensions already introduced. The 'givens' provide tensions and paradoxes, which the individual encounters in work within the four dimensions of human existence; the physical/Umwelt, social/ Mitwelt, personal/Eigenwelt and spiritual/ Uberwelt realms. They also provide a way into exploring and addressing the core aspects – relatedness, uncertainty and anxiety – that are present in all the dimensions.

To explore a person's worldview and the values and beliefs which affect their choice of behaviour and their decision-making is to look at how they operate in these different 'existential dimensions'. Whilst remaining a grounded, authentic and secure individual, we all know that we do not always feel or act the same in all contexts. We will choose to share different aspects of ourselves with different people, choosing when and with whom to 'let or hair down' and who we trust enough to share our innermost thoughts with. Like a single-lens camera, different aspects of ourselves will be brought into the foreground in different contexts.

When working with a client, the nature of the contract with the coach may be that they will focus on one dimension, but if the coach ignores the other dimensions, they will not get a full picture of the client's worldview and so may miss important aspects of their 'being-in-the-world' which will impact on the coaching work. A client may also identify one or more of the dimensions which are underdeveloped and as a result may wish to give them some attention. All of these dimensions are at play as much in our professional as our personal lives.

One clear example of this, often featuring in business coaching, is the identification that the time and importance the individual is giving to their job is to the detriment of their relationship with others and self. It is not uncommon that the way a person is in one dimension works against how they are in another. It is important that this be identified. However, there is no expectation or requirement that, once identified, the individual should seek to change the balance. It is the client's responsibility to note it and take responsibility for making a change or choosing not to change.

This part of the coaching relationship may sound a little too close to psychotherapy for some people in the business world, so let us look briefly at how they differ.

Existential coaching and psychotherapy

Many business leaders have been suspicious of anything which was too close to therapy. Although the term 'therapeutic workplace coaching' is no longer unspeakable, it is worth explaining the difference between existential coaching and existential psychotherapy. They hold to the same philosophy, but the focus is different.

Existential psychotherapy is an established and well-respected modality. It is an approach to therapy which draws on existential philosophy and on the belief that inner conflict within a person is due to that individual's confrontation with the givens of existence – the inevitability of death, freedom and its attendant responsibility, existential loneliness and anxiety, and meaninglessness.

Not surprisingly, as the interest in coaching has developed, people have also chosen to look to existential thought as a framework for guiding a new coaching approach (van Deurzen & Hanaway, 2012; Hanaway & Reed, 2014; Hanaway, 2018; Jacob, 2019). Jacob (2019, p. 16) writes '*Existential coaching is an approach that is rooted in and informed by existential philosophy, a branch of philosophy concerned with questions of existence – that is, what it means to exist, to be human and to be alive in a world with other people*' and identifies that the existential coach '*typically not only explored these questions theoretically and philosophically, but will have made their own experiences with the inevitable struggles and challenges that living brings with it*'. Jacob suggests that an existentially minded coach lives the philosophy as well as using it in their practise and will be '*eager to live a full life and does not shy away from courageously facing life's many challenges*'. (ibid., p. 26) He offers a useful list of existential themes relevant to leaders and the role that coaching can play when working with such themes (Table 6.2).

Although existential coaching draws on the same philosophical foundations as existential psychotherapy, they are not offering the same thing. It is a very focused coaching approach which works very well in the business setting and is very useful at all stages of management and leadership development. Existential coaching is often more boundaried in its focus than psychotherapy. It can be more focused on one particular issue or goal, for example, difficult conversations, time management and work stress, whilst existential psychotherapy has more of a free reign to focus and explore the values, beliefs, choices and behaviours of any element of a client's life. These aspects will still enter into the coaching dialogue and will help identify why these dilemmas are causing the person difficulties, but they will be explored in relation to the agreed-upon area of focus as expressed within an agreed-upon, usually time-limited, context.

This is not to say that psychotherapy cannot be equally singular in its attention.

In addition, it is possible that an existential coaching client might gain therapeutic benefit from coaching. That is to say that the client might take what they have learnt in the specific context of the business coaching and translate this learning into other areas of their lives, for example, difficult conversations with colleagues may provide relevant learning to use in difficult conversations with friends and

Table 6.2 Existential themes in leadership, their relevance for those in managing positions and the role of coaching when working with such themes

Existential theme	Relevance to leaders	The role of coaching
Responsibility	Responsible for the organisation's success, people's jobs and customers' needs or even health and well-being (depending on the organisation).	Accepting responsibility for choices. Exploring the boundaries of personal responsibility. Creating the foundation for authentic decision-making.
Choice	Needs to make important choices on a regular basis that potentially affect many people.	Becoming aware of choices and their link to values and worldview.
Freedom	Economic situation and resulting financial clampdowns lead organisations to try to be as secure as possible. This means that instead of making meaningful decisions or dealing with critical issues, senior staff are signing off on minimal spending. This leads to a loss of freedom.	Exploring organisational absurdity but also awareness of ultimate freedom. Exploring options and consequences and creating conscious choices and acceptance of facticity.
Temporality	The job might not last, competitive environment, fast-moving (business) world. Cuts to resources, projects end, tasks end, people are made redundant.	Exploring attitude towards endings, fostering acceptance that it's a given.
Others	Expectations, competition, being watched and evaluated by 'strangers', needing to introduce change as part of the job (change that people often reject). Being 'above the herd' risks abandonment, rejection, judgment and difference.	Exploring the social world. How does the leader relate to others? Using the here and now and the present relationship to explore relations with others. Becoming clear on one's role and others' worldviews in relation to one's role and others' worldviews in relation to one's own.
Uncertainty	Economic instability. Successful leaders need to leap into uncertainty to maximise success and gain an edge on competitors; taking risks necessary to be successful. Yet, anxiety is considered a taboo in Western cultures.	Anxiety can be used. Practice staying alert to and mindful of the possibilities that uncertainty creates (new directions, different ways of engaging with staff, welcoming input and collaboration etc.) Sitting with anxiety and finding peace and strength in it.
Authenticity	Leader me versus at-home me, organisation's goals/values/worldview versus own goals/values/worldview.	Help noticing when s/he is stepping in and out of in/authentic state. Heightened awareness of self leads to more conscious choices, decision-making and behaviours.

(Continued)

Table 6.2 (Continued) Existential themes in leadership, their relevance for those in managing positions and the role of coaching when working with such themes

Existential theme	Relevance to leaders	The role of coaching
Meaning	Meaning is inter-relational, connected to what is going on across the leader's four worlds (no work-private separation) Questions leaders ask themselves: • What am I doing this for? • What am I bringing to this role, my team, the organisation? • Do I want to do this anymore and, if so, then how do I do it in a way that means something to me? • What am I here for if not to lead? • What kind of leader do I want to be and what kind of meaning does that hold for me?	Help to differentiate between meaning of life and meaning in every task, activity, conversation etc, review, create and determine the two. Accept that they are ever-changing and need to be re-evaluated and recreated on an ongoing basis. Be open to change.
Organisational absurdity	Often a point is reached where nothing in the organisation seems to make sense any more. And it often really doesn't. No consistency in decisions, ridiculous rules. Selfishness and greed etc. Leaders who try to make sense of it suffer.	Accept that there is no ultimate ground for meaning. Juggling absurdity of the organisation as a whole and meaning in projects in particular. Commitment is a choice; we make our own meaning. Accept that there is no ultimate ground for meaning.
Anxiety	Experiencing existential anxiety is inevitable, but leaders often try to block it for various reasons.	Embracing anxiety as a reminder to wake up and engage, to keep oneself at optimal engagement with life and open to one's reality. This can lead to better judgment and more conscious choices through raised awareness, as well as inspiring others and managing relationships better.
Conflict	Inner conflict (living up to demands or own standards). External conflict (see 'others').	Using the here and now/present relationship to explore relations with others.
Bad faith	Leaders often deny that they are also human beings facing fear, doubt, anxiety, guilt, dread, unease and absurdity. They think they are or should be Übermenschen (supermen). Defence mechanisms: keeping busy, inauthentic divide of self (can't bear silence or the space or time to think).	Enlighten them to the struggles of life and allow them to experience some acceptance of these difficult feelings and emotions; learn to accept the inevitability of inauthenticity and notice reasons for it (more conscious choice).

Source: Jacob, Y., 2019, An Introduction to Existential Coaching, 84–85, Routledge, Reproduced with permissions.

family. Through the coaching they may become clearer about what their values and beliefs are and therefore what might trigger negative reactions when these are perceived to be under attack.

The coaching may clarify what meaning they are taking from their work activities. If their life meaning is mainly coming from work, then they need to consider whether this is okay for them or not and identify necessary strategies for change or retention. If their reflections from the process are relevant to their personal life, this process takes place within the client, independently of the coaching relationship, as a potential by-product, without intervention or direct facilitation from the coach.

Existential coaching is similarly more boundaried in terms of the exploration of the areas and developmental phases of the client's life when compared to existential psychotherapy. While existential coaching honours the past, it is aware of its fundamental relevance in terms of providing a context in which our beliefs and values are established. However it isn't focused on exploring the development of this context, but focuses instead on how it is being played out in the here and now, to the benefit or detriment of the client, in their work context.

The existential coach is interested in exploring the implications of these values and the client's worldview on the client's current context and the future that the client is working towards. Values determine our behaviour. Some values, beliefs and behaviours may have served the client well up to this point, but their effectiveness and relevance need to be reconsidered. In keeping with the existential emphasis on choice and freedom, the existential coach will explore whether some change is required, and how the client will make that change and take responsibility for their choice.

Models of existential coaching

Leaders seeks to coach people to do their best. By doing this, a leader enables them to make better decisions, solve problems that are holding them back, learn new skills and progress in their careers.

Some people are fortunate enough to get formal training in coaching skills. However, many leaders have to develop this important skill themselves. The GROW model is a simple yet powerful framework for structuring most coaching or mentoring sessions (Table 6.3).

By setting goals which are inspiring and challenging, as well as specific, measurable and achievable in a realistic time frame, the GROW model successfully promotes confidence and self-motivation, leading to increased productivity and personal satisfaction. The Will element of the fourth stage in the model is the barometer of success. It relates to volition, desire and intention.

The model was originally developed in the 1980s by business coaches Graham Alexander, Alan Fine and John Whitmore. A good way of thinking about the GROW model is to think about how you plan a journey. First, you decide where you are going (the goal) and establish where you currently are (your current

Table 6.3 GROW model

GROW stands for		
Goal	What do you want?	Raises awareness and understanding of – Own aspirations
Current **R**eality	Where are you now?	Raises awareness and understanding of – Current situation and beliefs
Options (or Obstacles)	What could you do?	Raises awareness and understanding of – The possibilities and resources open to them
Will (or Way Forward)	What will you do?	Raises awareness and understanding of – The actions they want to take to achieve their personal and professional goals

reality). You then explore various routes (the options) to your destination. In the final step, establishing the will, you ensure that you are committed to making the journey and are prepared for the obstacles that you could meet on the way. GROW utilises a deceptively simple framework, yet provides a powerful tool to highlight, elicit and maximise inner potential, through a series of sequential coaching conversations.

In exploring the Goal, the coach will agree the topic for discussion and the specific objective for the session. If appropriate, they will also agree to a long-term aim. In the Reality phase, the client will be invited to undertake a process of self-assessment and offer specific examples for feedback. Assumptions will be checked and irrelevant history discarded. The coach will then move the client on to explore their options, inviting them to identify a full range of options and then to make choices between those options. In the final stage the client will be future focused and commit to action, identify any potential obstacles and agree to and plan any support they may need in taking their plans into reality.

Some people find acronyms like GROW very helpful in holding ideas in the mind. Unlike GROW models, existential approaches are not linear or chronological. The existential coach is not thrown by diversion but welcomes the creativity of the client, whilst remaining alert to the job in hand and the goal or goals which the client identifies. These goals may be fixed and externally driven, as in much business coaching, or there may be potential for more fluidity, with the possibility of goals being dropped or reframed as the client becomes more aware of what holds most meaning for them.

As existential approaches are not prescriptive, coaches and those leaders using a coaching approach need to formulate their own unique model of existential coaching. In training existential coaches I am often asked for an easily remembered existential model. Together with Jamie Reed (Hanaway, 2018), we developed two such models: CREATE, which focuses on the process involved in an existential coaching encounter (the name reflecting existential coaching's commitment to a creative, not prescriptive encounter), and MOVER, which focuses on the dynamic and core philosophical elements of the approach.

CREATE takes one through the start of the coaching relationship, starting at the first Contact, and looks at the development of the psychological and physical meeting of the coach and client and the setting up of the coaching contract. It looks at the physical, social, psychological and spiritual aspects of this early stage, thus covering all the existential dimensions.

From there, it moves on to look at Responsibility. A key existential belief is concerned with taking responsibility for one's own decisions and their implications. The model looks at the different foci of responsibility for coach and client. Put simply, the coach is responsible for the process, holding any agreed-upon boundaries, keeping the client's goals in mind, holding the line between coaching and therapy and signposting any additional help or support which may be needed by the client. The client is responsible for the content, what they choose to tell and what they choose not to reveal, ensuring that the work remains authentic and taking personal responsibility for implementing agreed future action or not.

Having established a trusting and clear working alliance, the coach moves on to the next stage. In this stage, the aim is to Explore the client's worldview using the existential dimensions and core concepts as a framework. The coach is not asking direct questions about these, but using active listening skills to hear what the client is telling them, usually indirectly, about these existential issues. Through this exploration, the coach learns what is of importance to this client and can hold this knowledge of the client's values in mind, whilst checking the meaningfulness of any proposed future action plan.

Moving to Awareness, this stage marks the growing awareness of a client for how well their current position fits with their values and need for meaning. This awareness may be unsettling and require the client to look at some uncomfortable truths. They may need to decide on whether to stay in a post and take steps to increase the meaning within it, or they may decide that the post will never provide them with the meaning they need. They may still choose to stay in the post but look for more meaning outside work, or they may identify another position which appears to have the potential to be more meaningful. Without this awareness, which may be painful, it is impossible for them to move on in any authentic way.

Once the awareness is present, it leads on to the stage where the work begins to focus on Tuning out from the exploration of the worldview, and the client and coach focus on what this increased personal insight means for the client's future actions. At this stage the coaching sessions focus back on the specific issues and goals of the initial contract. The exploration stage should have enabled the client to see different ways of addressing these issues, using an increased awareness of what is fundamentally important to the client as a unique entity in the world, yet also addressing the implications any decisions may have for others, including the organisation.

Once all these stages are completed, the coach and client have to formulate a meaningful and clear Ending to the coaching relationship. This may be particularly difficult for some clients who find it difficult to build trusting, confidential

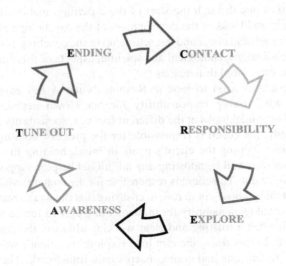

Figure 6.1 CREATE model. (From Hanaway & Reed, 2012).

relationships and may be unhappy about letting go of a successful and trusted coaching relationship (Figure 6.1).

Any coaching relationship is about movement. It is usually focused on facilitating the client to move from a situation or mindset which has become stuck or sedimented in some way. CREATE focuses on the activity of the coach and client during the session, whilst MOVER focuses more explicitly on the existential and more philosophical elements of the coaching session, flowing from the core existential concepts to explore how they can form a dynamic framework for the coach's work with the client (Figure 6.2).

The search for Meaning lies at the heart of existential thinking, so is very prominent in this model. In coaching it is important to understand the meaning that the client is giving to the coaching relationship. What are they looking for? What do they understand about the nature of the coaching contract? Before a productive coaching process can be established, there is a need to clarify what meaning is being given to the process and what meaning the client is currently experiencing in relation to any dilemma they bring to coaching. A common reason for people to feel unsettled in work is because something which had been meaningful has lost its meaning.

During the temporality of life, we encounter many obstacles to our free will and action, and equally will be presented with many opportunities, some of which, given that we have freedom, we may chose to ignore, and others which may inspire us to action. Within existential coaching, it is important to explore the client's perception of potential Obstacles. Often the obstacles can be reframed as Opportunities. Coaches work with clients to explore the obstacles in a specific temporary dilemma they are struggling with. Through reflective exploration,

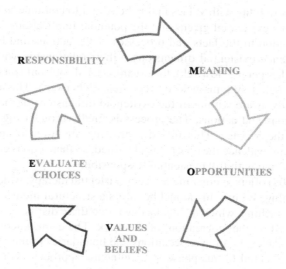

Figure 6.2 MOVER model. (From Hanaway & Reed, 2012).

they identify not only any such obstacles, but also any opportunities which may be presented for new and creative action. Through the coaching, clients seek to identify ways of negotiating their way under, over or through these obstacles.

It is important for the coach to explore all options and strategies available within the context of a deep understanding of the client's values and beliefs. If ways forward are identified which ignore or go against the client's values, then the client is likely to find it difficult to follow through on the agreed-upon actions. If they ignore their anxiety and go ahead anyway, it is possible that they will be subject to strong feelings of anguish, guilt and confusion when the task is completed. To carry out a task which works against one's values may leave a reflective person with a deep sense of inauthenticity, which for some may be difficult to live with. In existential coaching it is an ethical requirement for the coach to check whether the proposed action works with or against the client's value system, and to ensure that the client has sufficient space to consider the 'fit' of the action in relation to their values and the implications of that action. It is not a prerequisite that for the action to take place it must align with the client's values. What is required is that the client reflect on whether there is a conflict which makes the action impossible, or whether the challenge can be accommodated and worked with. To move forward authentically, the client needs to acknowledge this to be the case, own their decision to go forward with the action or not and take **R**esponsibility for the implications of that decision.

Taking on the responsibility and ownership of the decision can only follow on from an honest **E**valuation of the individual's decision-making process. Once the meaning, values and obstacles have been explored and some potential ways forward identified, these need to be evaluated. It is important to consider how the proposed action fits with values and beliefs, and to continue to explore these in relation to the existential givens and the potential implications. This needs to be done in relation to the facts and processes of the actions and how they will impact the client's existential dimensions – their relationship with themselves (Eigenwelt), other people (Mitwelt), the organisational environment (Umwelt) and the important belief systems held by the client (Uberwelt). The aim is for the client to be fully aware within all the existential dimensions of the implications of their decisions and actions. The process is finally brought together through summarising the journey. This includes drawing attention to any paradoxes, ambiguity or ambivalence the coach has identified, so that actions can be taken in full knowledge and with full existential Responsibility.

Spinelli (2007) offers another model from existential therapy, which can equally apply to coaching. Within this model he offers a structural model of the process of therapy or coaching, which he breaks down into three distinct phases. The first phase is focused on the 'cocreation' of the work. The central activity here is to explore and make explicit the expectations and boundaries of the relationship for both parties. Essential to this phase is an authentic approach with an attitude of openness and honesty so that a shared understanding and grounding is established for going forward. From there, the Spinelli model moves on to the examination of the challenges provoked for the client by the coaching relationship itself. In this way, the client's worldview and issues of relatedness are brought to light and explored 'intensely' in the context of their relationship to the existential coach. As a consequence of exploring and potentially reconfiguring some of the client's perspectives, there may well be implications and new possibilities disclosed for the client's wider worldview. This represents the bridge, as Spinelli describes it, for closing down the coaching relationship. As a model it focuses more on the coaching relationship than do the MOVER and CREATE models but can also be used effectively in the business context.

As Spinelli also points out, existential therapy or coaching are not in any way linear and so cannot be reduced to a process as easy as 1-2-3. Instead, as the MOVER and CREATE models of coaching suggest, the process is more cyclical than linear in nature. Existential coaches look to work intensely with their clients to establish the core concerns of their client's perspective, values and beliefs in relation to their desired focus for the coaching. In all of the above, the coach will seek to adhere to an existential framework.

Peltier (2009) came up with 10 guidelines for existential coaching which can help to provide the baseline from which the work develops. First, our uniqueness as individuals needs to be honoured. Implicit in this is the need for coaches, and indeed the same could be seen as being true for leaders, to know their staff and to uncover those unique aspects of each individual. If we value this uniqueness, then it follows that we encourage people to figure things out in their own way, rather than directing them. This can feel threatening to some leaders as it opens up the possibility of their views and desires being questioned and alternatives being proposed.

At the same time as honouring individuality, we need to acknowledge that we do not exist alone in the world, and so there is a need to create and sustain authentic relationships. Peltier emphases the value of taking responsibility and encouraging choice, in line with existential thinking, on the interrelatedness of freedom and responsibility. He invites coaches and clients to engage with uncertainty through welcoming and appreciating the absurd, and to engage with conflict and confrontation, as they are inevitable aspects of the human condition. Leadership and business generally often have a very difficult relationship with uncertainty. When writing business plans we choose to behave as though the future is certain. Peltier, whilst acknowledging the need to anticipate anxiety and defensiveness, calls on us to be action oriented and to 'get going' despite the anxiety and absence of certainty, and to go ahead and commit to *something*. This call brings to mind Kierkegaard's invitation, in 'Concluding Unscientific Postscript', to take a 'leap of faith' instead of always seeking a certainty, which is impossible to achieve.

Clients can expect an existential coach to encourage them to speak up for themselves and the values they hold and not to be treated as if they fit into a pre-established model. This requires a creative dialogue where clients take charge of their own exploration and are helped to think in new ways about making choices and decisions in their lives. The coach will help the client to clarify for themselves who they think they are, where they are and where they want to go in life. Clients will be encouraged to probe a little further and deeper and to challenge their assumptions about their lives, themselves, other people and the world they live in. They will have an opportunity to tackle the conflicts in their lives and understand not only how they contribute to creating some of these but also how to face up to conflicts and surpass them, by learning about reciprocity, generosity and empathy. They will consider dialectical principles and the ways in which they may make more of the paradoxes of human existence, using the ebb and flow of their lives to create movement for themselves. In recognising their own ideology, in the form of their unspoken assumptions, prejudices, values, deep-seated beliefs and their predictive framework of human existence, clients can tackle some of the distortions that have obscured their vision and so increase their capacity for widening their perspective on their life and on human existence in general.

Through clarifying their personal philosophy, they can feel better able to be tested and challenged and potentially abandon old destructive habits and replace them with new and more creative and meaningful ways of proceeding in life, through engaging in a meaningful purpose and project. This approach works equally well within the professional as well as the personal context and fits well with the task of coaching leaders. Leadership is not a static state, indeed, like life itself, it is temporal. As we know, an existential leadership model holds at its heart the understanding of temporality, leading to the search for meaning and the authentic holding of values. For many leaders there will be times when personal and organisational values are in conflict, leading to feelings of inauthenticity and bad faith. In the seemingly hard-nosed business world, existential themes and dilemmas are often at the heart of the work the client brings to coaching, although they are often accessed through the exploration of the more concrete dilemmas and themes which the client more readily presents, and which may come to the fore at different stages in their leadership journey.

People move through many stages in their leadership careers. Wherever an individual is on that path, they have to confront the uncertainty of whether that direction will continue along the same upward trajectory. They may feel very uncertain about their own future and that of the organisation and yet be aware that those they are leading are looking to them to provide certainty and stability in order to lessen existential anxiety.

Each step on the leadership route throws up new existential challenges. Many organisations employ coaches to work with individuals in whom they see leadership potential, with leaders new to the leadership role, with those changing the context of their leadership or the nature of the teams they are leading, through to working with those preparing to leave their leadership position and take on new challenges, including the huge challenge of retirement or redundancy.

Each phase of leadership requires the leader to engage with different aspects of uncertainty and levels of existential anxiety. Leaders have often gained their position by moving from a position of some comfort, where they have exhibited their competence and had that recognised by others, into a new, challenging and uncertain context. Initially, their self-esteem may be high and they may believe they have a high level of certainty and confidence in their abilities. Many believe that a leadership role will inevitably bring greater control and increased freedom. There may be a greater opportunity to make more money, find new challenges and so on by gaining greater influence and power in the organisation. However, existentially we enjoy no more or no less real control of our lives regardless of the position we hold. All that is created is an increasing amount of behaviour seeking to 'evidence' control. There is hardly any leadership post where one is not 'controlled' by someone or something else.

Remaining authentic in a leadership promotion can be extremely confusing and challenging and may lead to a questioning of one's self-concept. Many new leaders enjoyed their previous work, liked the person they were able to be in the role and felt confident in their abilities. They may have enjoyed the camaraderie of feeling part of a team. The move to leadership can feel a very lonely one in which many people feel they cannot be their true self. They feel they must maintain a confident, strong and authoritative presence. A case in point is that of Justin, who as the youngest member of a partnership group had felt able to express any uncertainty or worries to his older peers. On promotion he soon discovered that although his peers had all congratulated him on the appointment, they held very mixed feelings about his promotion over them. Some were invested in him failing, and others were just unwilling to help him by sharing ideas or helping him problem-solve.

A new leader, like Justin, may feel that they are required to make a Faustian pact in which they sacrifice a sense of belonging and confidence in exchange for status, perceived power and influence. Of course most of us want all these things. One of the ontological, universal human shared givens is that contradictions and paradoxes, which are irresolvable, are constantly with us. They can be called instincts, ontological givens, inclinations or intuitions. Human beings are thrown into this world to find meaning through aspiring to something, being ambitious and achieving something which may leave a legacy. At the same time, as soon as we achieve our aspirations we might become bored, exhausted, worn out and apathetic, and understand that new aspirations need to be created. These states of being may be accompanied by paradoxes between belonging and isolation, security versus risk taking, apathy versus ambition, being honest and straightforward and acting in a more dishonest and complex way. An existential coach will seek to enable the client to see the paradoxes inherent in their dilemma and facilitate the client's exploration of their values and priorities. Understanding they cannot have everything, the client can then use their freedom to choose and take responsibility for their choice. They may need to choose between ambition and a sense of security and belonging. As Strasser and Strasser (1997, p. 69) pointed out, humans engage in a *'perennial search for safety and security in a world that is replete with uncertainties and unpredictability is one of the paradoxes of our existence'*. Entering a leadership position will not shield us from this.

An existential coach will help the leader gain a more in-depth understanding of self through exploring their existential dimensions. The coach and client will discuss what is important for the client in their physical (Umwelt), social (Mitwelt), psychological (Eigenwelt) and spiritual (Uberwelt) dimensions. Often these dimensions can be in conflict with one another, and as humans we have to live with our own paradoxes and ambivalences. We need to accept uncertainty and that our lives are paradoxical. We may want conflicting things. We may want to be a good team player, yet value our autonomy. We may relate to our body positively, perhaps seeing it as the mechanism through which we carry out our decisions and yet we may be faced with the decline of that body through illness, accident or age. Something that we once felt proud of may become something in which we feel shame, or we may be frustrated by its limitations.

In working as a coach with Justin, I saw a clear example of many of these challenges being played out. Justin was in his mid-thirties and had made a spectacular rise in an established and highly regarded global company. His fellow partners had considered him Amanda's (the CEO) 'blue-eyed boy' and were not surprised when Amanda informed them that she was taking a year's break to work on a new project and was promoting Justin to the CEO role whilst she moved to more of a silent partner role. Justin was delighted and felt very confident that he would make a huge success of the new role.

One of the first things he realised on taking up the new position was the difference in his relationship to the other partners, whom he had considered to be his friends, and with whom he had socialised outside of the work environment. The new role meant a change in his 'relatedness' to colleagues and others within the organisation. His relationship to his **Mitwelt** or social existential dimension was changed. This involved both gains and losses. He was no longer seen as part of the group and there was no other person at his level in the hierarchy, so he was plunged into a new sense of loneliness, whilst at the same time experiencing power over those who were now beneath him in the hierarchy. Of course, having power over someone also distances them from you and isolates you further as you can choose to make life easy or hard for them, to criticise or praise them, and ultimately to determine their future in the organisation.

Amanda had declared that she wanted to give Justin his freedom to do things his way without having her breathing down his neck and so intended to leave him to get on with it, declaring she had full trust in his abilities. This made it difficult for Justin to remain authentic. His own sense of self, his **Eigenwelt**, was challenged. He was expected to be dynamic, confident, certain and in control, yet he no longer experienced himself as being any of these things. He felt small, scared, alone and uncertain about how things would go. He was full of ontological anxiety. Unfortunately he did not feel that he could voice any of these concerns. He was faced with seeing himself in a different way, where his vulnerabilities were to the forefront in his mind. He did not want to expose these aspects to the partners. He was beginning to reframe his relationship with them, no longer experiencing them as supportive friends and colleagues but as potential threats to his current position. He may have held hierarchical power over them, yet they held the power to help him achieve his objectives or to sabotage them. They also held the power of over his ability to feel a sense of belonging or of being alone. The freedom Amanda had given to him brought with it large expectations, and he began to realise the level of responsibility which accompanied that freedom, leading to increased anxiety. He was faced with many choices and decisions which he was expected to make alone.

His promotion meant that Justin had reached the leadership level he had always longed for much sooner than he had ever expected. This had initially boosted his self-esteem. His position now matched his long held self-concept but this self-concept was now under threat. He felt proud of his achievement but his position felt very vulnerable in a way he had not previously experienced under Amanda's benevolent eye. He also realised that the promotion required him to leave behind the group in which he had felt 'very at home' and strong and confident, at the same time as Amanda became absent to him. This brought some uncomfortable truths and paradoxes to the surface, not just about his relationship to others, but also in relation to self – what he thought he valued and needed most and what in fact he discovered to be the case. For the first time, he had to consider what was meaningful for him.

He needed to concern himself with the **Uberwelt**, his spiritual dimension which provides a place where we seek to find meaning against the threat of meaninglessness. I have already written about the centrality of meaning in existential thinking and the increased need for many of us to find meaning through our work. In his new position Justin began to reflect on what was meaningful for him and to ask himself a series of existential questions. He found himself pondering such thoughts as: Did status matter more than belonging? 'Who' was he as CEO? How did the role affect his behaviour? Did he like himself more or less in the new role? Was his working life meaningful to him? Did he believe in what he was doing? At the beginning of our coaching work, all these existential questions made him nauseous.

Even his relationship to the **Umwelt**, his physical dimension: his environment and own body, was brought into question. Before his promotion he had enjoyed being in the office he shared with a colleague. He felt safe there and kept a tidy desk, which he believed reflected the way in which he was in control of his workload. In his new role he had his own office with no one to chat to during the day. He felt trapped. Until recently, he was rarely ill and would often stop off to join friends at the gym on his way home after work. Now he was plagued with headaches. He often felt physically weak and dizzy. He experienced himself as being in a battle with his body. His desk was hardly visible underneath a stack of files and bits of paper that made him feel out of control. He no longer went to the gym after work; if he went anywhere, it was to the pub on his own. Weekends had previously proved a bit boring for him but now they were a welcome marker that he had survived another week and he began to find he got some relief from his worries when out on a solitary country walk, a new activity for him. Yet even the walks were accompanied with guilt that he was not catching up with his workload. Unfortunately, the other way he sought to cope with his anxieties was through an increased use of alcohol, more often than not when he was on his own. His weight increased and he no longer felt comfortable in his own skin.

These changes put him in touch with the existential concerns of time and temporality. Not too long ago, he had measured time by how quickly he could get to the top in his career, marking each milestone he passed on the career route. Now he had the sense of time passing too quickly for him to do everything the role required of him. He hadn't worried about what he wanted to do after achieving the CEO post; he had felt confident that success would follow success. Now, he couldn't allow himself to think beyond the next day, as all he saw in the future was a dark void in which he was exposed as inadequate. He became more aware of the temporality of things, including his own existence, sensing that he would not occupy his current role for long and seeing the toll the worry was taking on his body. This put him in touch with the vulnerability and temporality of his body and with the inevitability of death.

Amanda stayed in the background, but at the same time was closely monitoring Justin's work. She began to be very concerned by some of Justin's decisions. She did not like it when he chose to do some things in a different way to how she would have done them. She disapproved of many of his business decisions and was very critical of what she saw as his lack of success and the slow pace in which he did things. Without any prior discussion she returned to the CEO post and demoted Justin back to his previous position.

Justin experienced this as a public humiliation. He was no longer on the upward trajectory but felt cast down lower than the position he had occupied before his promotion. He felt ashamed and embarrassed and believed that his peers were laughing at him behind his back. He felt powerless and in a state of constant anxiety.

In the coaching we were able to explore Justin's engagement with each of the existential dimensions and many of the key areas of existential thought – freedom and responsibility, meaning, authenticity and relatedness.

The prevailing issue, as Justin identified it, sat in the Mitwelt or social dimension. He had lost connection with those he had considered his colleagues and friends. He was left in a place of loneliness, with a sense of emptiness and void which was highlighted in his lack of meaningful relationships as well as being an internal problem. We identified that increased relatedness to others would not on its own address existential loneliness, as we can often feel it most profoundly when we are with others. He began to consider what meaning he attached to relationships. Uncomfortably for him, he recognised that until now, he had judged relationships by the extent to which they enhanced his journey to the top in the business world. He had put time and energy only into those relationships which he believed would benefit him. This had left him little time to develop friendships or romantic relationships outside of work. Giving voice to this surprised Justin and he recognised that he did not want to remain 'that kind of person'. He recalled how important friendships had been to him growing up and throughout his youth and felt this had only changed when he had entered the business world. He believed he needed to seriously consider his next choices. He could continue in his current type of work and give more energy to creating and retaining rich relationships with work colleagues and making more time to develop relationships outside work. Alternatively, he could change careers and move to something which was more person centred.

This led him to reassess what made life meaningful for him. For many years he would have said that his meaning was created through his business success. It seemed to address some of his existential anxiety and uncertainty as he was choosing to follow a very clear career trajectory, and he rarely, if ever, stopped to ask if it was something he still wanted to do. It was a shock to him that, having achieved the success he desired so much, he found no meaning in his new position and instead of feeling a sense of security, pride and achievement he was frozen with fear. It seemed that he had put time and energy into something which no longer felt worth achieving. He realised that, rather like Sartre's waiter in *Being and Nothingness*, he had merely donned the uniform of a CEO without considering whether it was a good fit, suited him or even felt comfortable. Just like the waiter, he had *'applied himself to chaining his movements as if they were mechanisms, the one regulating the other'*. He was playing the part of being a CEO and had lost any sense of his authentic self. He had been faced with a number of paradoxes; he enjoyed the status but disliked how this set him aside from others, he had felt confident that he could do the job and yet he failed, he had felt grateful to Amanda for the opportunity but now wondered whether he had been set up to fail.

The crisis of 'failing' allowed him to review and take responsibility for his choices. He was not stuck with them. He had succeeded in his previous post and enjoyed the work. His self-esteem had pushed him to keep looking for promotion and now his self-esteem made it hard for him to return to his previous post or to leave the company for a lower-status job. Amanda and his colleagues were keen to keep Justin in the company but not as CEO. Justin had to consider the risk to his self-esteem in staying in the company where people were aware he had not succeeded as CEO, and the threat to his self-esteem in stepping away and taking a different job, perhaps one with less perceived status.

Justin realised that he had stopped reflecting on his values and beliefs and had proceeded forward on autopilot from one promotion to the next. Since starting working in the company, his wants, needs and values had become nonreflected 'sedimentations'. In the coaching we explored the potential to stir some of his sedimentations. Both Spinelli (1997, 2007) and Strasser (1999) stress the importance of re-examining sedimented values and emotions, checking out their meaning and validity in the immediate situation, in order to be best placed to make authentic decisions. In exploring these with Justin, he came to realise that he had not sufficiently interrogated his own values. He came to understand that what he valued and needed was a sense of achievement. This had become tied up in his mind with the idea of promotion on a straight line of career progression. He now saw that these were not the same thing and that there were many areas of life and possible activities which could provide him with that sense of achievement which made life meaningful for him.

In the exploration of Justin's Eigenwelt, we focused on his personal psychological dimension, his inner world, helping him to explore his paradoxes and the tension between integrity and disintegration. The Eigenwelt is also concerned with the private and intimate relations which had become absent in Justin's life. He had always presumed that he would marry and have children. This image was part of his picture of 'being a business success'. He did not need much prompting to describe what his wife might look like, the style of house he would live in and the make of the two cars in the drive, but when asked to describe how he might bring all these things to reality, he was aware that life as he was currently living it did not leave time for him to meet someone.

Justin began to realise he could not have everything and needed to have a clear sense of who he was in order to move from his current state of despair and confusion. He found it to be a difficult task to decide what was most important to him and what would allow him to regain his self-esteem and sense of authentic living. Each possible choice contained a potential gain and a potential loss. He needed to take a leap of faith and move forward authentically. He considered who he had believed himself to be, and who he truly was. He was also able to engage with his transience and his own potentialities.

Engaging with the truth that time was passing, Justin realised that due to the pressure of work he had not taken a holiday for three years, and he had not tested his potentialities outside of the narrow constraints of his job. He began to tell me about his love of surfing and mountain climbing, neither of which he had engaged in since the move to his current company. He spoke of the sense of achievement in reaching the top of a mountain or coming safely to shore having ridden a massive wave. As he spoke he recognised that he would never feel that high visceral level of achievement in his current work and he realised how much he missed it and how alive he had felt. Those activities had addressed his Umwelt needs by engaging him with the environment and the power of his physical body. They addressed the Mitwelt as he enjoyed these activities in the company of others. They were meaningful and so enriched his Uberwelt and his self-concept and lifted him above the day to day. Overall on the psychological level of the Eigenwelt when engaged in these activities, he felt positive and hopeful.

So, we return briefly to the nauseating existential questions that Justin had found himself facing at the start of the coaching. When considering whether status mattered more than belonging, he came to believe that whilst needing to feel that he was achieving things, achievement did not need to carry an externally validated status. He understood that he did not enjoy being alone and valued sharing his enthusiasm and activities with others. He thought about '"who" he was as CEO' and did not like what he saw. He had tried to use his power to guard against his self-doubt and vulnerabilities and felt he had lost himself in the process, becoming a person he did not particularly like and whose behaviour did not match his values. When pondering whether his working life was meaningful to him and whether he believed in what he was doing, he realised that this was an uncomfortable question he had consciously chosen not to address. The situation forced him to confront this, and he concluded that the work itself held little meaning, but that progression and achievement did. In understanding this, he began to consider how this might be achieved elsewhere.

Justin took a leave of absence from the company for a year. I later learnt that he had used the year to travel and pursue all the outdoor activities he so loved. He met his future wife on these travels. Together they set up a surfing centre and he chose not to return to the company when the year finished. In his desire to live authentically, he had taken his leap of faith and it had paid off. He was now the CEO of his own company without suffering the losses he had previously experienced in that role.

As we have seen, promotion usually requires a change of function and the acquisition of new skills. Each move up the leadership ladder will inevitably mean spending less time in operational delivery and more time managing. Initially this phase is akin to an ironic game of existential snakes and ladders. In the desire to experience more control, more success and greater certainty, we must first expose ourselves to greater uncertainty and more anxiety by confronting what we don't know about ourselves in our new role. If this is unbearable, then we may move into attempting to *play* the part and we may end up in a state of Sartrean 'Bad Faith'. We can find ourselves faced with the same existential questions Justin faced in the challenge to remain authentic.

Authenticity and its pursuit in existential terms require to us to take responsibility for the unique nature of our being as the key challenge of living. This includes the capacity to attempt to be true to one's self. *'Behaving authentically means acting in accordance with one's values, preferences, and needs as opposed to acting merely to please others or to attain rewards or avoid punishments through acting "falsely"…. Authenticity is not reflected in a compulsion to be one's true self, but rather in the free expression of core feelings, motives and inclinations'* Kernis (2003, p. 16).

Prior to moving into any sort of management position, it can be relatively easy to behave in a way that is likely to please the organisation and thus help to gain promotion by 'playing the game'. Sartre was interested in this use of playing and 'being in a certain way' as a strategy for avoiding uncertainty and our sense of 'nothingness'. However, when promoted, we are under increased gaze of others, with the increased awareness of how we are perceived. Under such observation we must accept a greater degree of responsibility and accountability for our actions. This responsibility in turn discloses our anxiety and calls us to question our authenticity.

Collectively or in combination, these phenomena can represent a real challenge for the newly promoted individual. Initially, this uncertainty can result in a period of isolation and limited sense of safety. Having access to a safe space through coaching can be of invaluable benefit and provide an opportunity to respond to some of these existential experiences and questions.

Moving up the leadership ladder brings with it a more visual line of responsibility. As a leader one is open to observation and criticism, often from an ill-informed standpoint. There is likely to be a marked increase in the impact that one's decisions now make to the organisation and to those employed within it. The decisions being made at this level can have profound strategic and/or financial implications for the organisation and a life-changing impact on the careers of some individuals. As a consequence, there is likely to be a far greater level of visibility within the organisation to the outcomes of these decisions, for better or for worse. This can bring increased pressure for the individual. There is nowhere to hide and a leader must live with the awareness that they are under constant scrutiny, not just from stakeholders and customers, but also, perhaps somewhat paradoxically, from those whom the leader has power over structurally – those they employ. Thus, the expected or hoped-for increase in freedom is seen as having a very visible impact, carrying greater responsibility.

Given the potential size of the team that a senior leader is likely to be responsible for, their core contact with the operational delivery within the business is inevitably going to be mainly through others. This engagement is one step away from those delivering the work and may remove the leader further from the meaning which originally attracted them to the organisation. They may miss the satisfaction of direct customer contact and a more immediate engagement with the impact of the work.

However, for a business to be successful and meaningful it needs both strategic leadership and operational delivery. A strategy, which a leader may have spent months developing, is without meaning if there is no one to implement it. Equally work without a purpose or a plan may be little more than a Sisyphean project in which workers feel punished by the requirement to engage in a seemingly meaningless activity, which feels like pushing a large rock up on a steep hill, only to find it rolling back on nearing the top.

This separation between strategy and operational activity can result in a lessening of empathy and of the ability to consider the impact of decisions on other individuals. Some leaders would claim that this is an essential part of being a leader. Leaders often have to discipline, demote or even sack people and this is a harder task if one allows oneself to engage in the implications for that individual. In my own business life I have had to do all of these things. I have tried to carry them out in a way which was in accord with my values and beliefs, and through which I could remain authentic.

Sometimes this meant I was faced with having to address my own sedimented values, as in the example I shared earlier with the senior manager who asked to be micromanaged. This required me to make a choice between two strongly held values: my desire to encourage autonomy and creativity in members of my staff team and my desire to provide an excellent, timely service to clients.

In a different example, in which I found it easier to remain true to my values, I needed to dismiss a member of staff who was not competent in carrying out her duties. In my view this was not her fault. As an Afro-Caribbean woman, she had been appointed by the previous leader in a crude attempt to improve the racial diversity in the company for the purpose of better equal opportunity monitoring figures. I believed the organisation had a responsibility to her, but to keep her in post was not consistent with carrying out our responsibility to the client. I sought to hold to both my perceived responsibilities, as I saw them, by arranging for her to job shadow posts in which I felt her strengths would be better suited. By the date we had agreed for her to leave, she had secured a job in one of the companies where she had job shadowed and in which her strengths could be fully utilised, so providing a more meaningful and satisfying work experience for her. Some time after she left, I received a letter in which she thanked me for 'sacking her' stating that she had been deeply unhappy in the post, knowing that she could not successfully undertake the work expected of her and feeling that she was letting down her colleagues, her clients, the organisation, herself and me. She was very happy and successful in the new post, working in an area she felt passionate about and confident in her contributions.

It would have been helpful to discuss these decisions with a coach who would have helped me to focus on my own existential needs. I did not need a coach to take me through the process of dismissing someone and ensuring that all procedures were correct to avoid any subsequent tribunal, I knew that already and could check out any legalities easily. I needed to explore any ambiguities in my thinking, to identify any tensions across my values and beliefs and to ensure that by the end of the process I knew I had remained authentic in my actions. At that time, there were no existential coaches and so, as is true for many leaders, I developed my own internal existential coach and set aside time to 'have sessions with myself' to examine these issues and to reflectively act, own and take responsibility for the implications of my decisions for the individuals concerned, for the reputation of the organisation, for the outcome for clients and for my own self concept.

Being removed from the operational, and the relatedness to those at that level, can also mean that a leader is more removed from the sense of satisfaction that someone in a different position feels when their part of the process is successfully completed. I have often envied people who make things, builders, carpenters, gardeners and so on, as at some point they and others can stand back and admire a completed project. At a senior leadership level it can be harder to access that piece of personal pride and satisfaction as the leader is dependent on everyone else doing their jobs well for the project to be a success. Although success is shared, failure is often placed firmly at the door of the leader.

When coaching the founding director of a successful global company, our focus was on how she could find that feeling of satisfaction. The company was highly successful, yet the team of partners was very vocally critical of her whenever anything went wrong at any level. This was so upsetting to her that she considered closing the company down. Through our work she identified that she needed some acknowledgment from the partners that she had set up the company and her efforts had enabled them to earn considerable sums of money, whilst giving them secure employment. She acknowledged that like anyone, not all her decisions were successful, but she looked to the partners to acknowledge that they were taken with the intention of developing the company and making it more successful, and that the only person who lost out financially through these initiatives was herself. We considered how others might perceive her, and she began to understand that as a woman in a male-dominated industry she had sought to come across as tough and unemotional. She had avoided discussion and collaboration, as she was fearful that this might result in her being seen as weak and unable to make decisions on her own. Her work persona had resulted in her living inauthentically, or in a state of Sartrean 'bad faith'. On the surface she had acted as an automaton, or in the *role* of 'founding director', so it was not so surprising that the partners were relating to her in that way rather than as a human being with vulnerabilities, emotions, hopes and fears. In order to have a sense of achievement, she needed others to reflect this and give her positive feedback in addition to any constructive criticism she may justifiably have received. She decided 'to expose more of her real self' to the team of partners, to invite them to contribute ideas for the development of the company, and openly express disappointment, but not always to blame her if things did not go according to plan.

Existential challenges are present in each leadership phase. This is just as true at the end of a leadership role as it is at the beginning. As time and temporality are so key to existential thinking, it is not unexpected that the coming of retirement presents important existential as well as practical considerations.

What we mean by retirement is inconsistent. Ekerdt (2010, p. 70) saw the designation of retirement status as *'famously ambiguous because there are multiple overlapping criteria by which someone might be called retired, including career cessation, reduced work effort, pension receipt, or self-report'*. Adding possible confusion to the self-report definition of retirement is the fact that individuals can 'unretire' or 'reretire' by rejoining the workforce or starting new careers. Many people are now running a 'portfolio' of jobs following 'retirement' from a full-time post. This allows them more control of their time and presents a variety of meaningful challenges.

Historically, retirement is a relatively new phenomenon. Throughout most of history, individuals continued to work until they were simply no longer physically able to. It was not until the industrial revolution, the creation of Social Security and the wider availability of company pension benefits in the first half of the twentieth century that individuals were able to cease paid employment while they were still otherwise able to work. For this reason, it is only recently that attention has been given to the psychological dynamics of retirement in relation to individual, group, organisational and societal levels (Beehr & Bennett, 2007; Shultz & Henkens, 2010).

People are living longer and so spending a longer time in retirement. Previously, retirement planning was focused on physical and financial issues rather than the psychological aspects of retirement. This was due partly to the fact that many retirement presentations and workshops were provided by financial institutions. Interest in the psychological aspects of retirement has increased with the awareness that financial security in retirement is but one important element and that retirement brings with it psychological and existential dilemmas.

Although the authentic felt experience, and the circumstances, of retirement are always unique, we can still draw out some universal issues which are likely to arise for most people. Osborne (2012) suggests these issues include partial identity disruption, decision paralysis, diminished self trust, experience of a postretirement void, the search for meaningful engagement in society, development of a retirement/life structure, the confluence of aging and retirement, death anxiety, the critical nurturing of social relationships and self-actualisation. It is clear that these sit within the existential dimensions (social, spiritual, physical and psychological) and include many of the main existential concerns – meaningfulness; time and temporality; identity, self-concept and self-esteem; freedom, decision-making and responsibility; existential anxiety and uncertainty. Retirement brings into sharp relief some psychological and existential questions which it may have been possible to ignore earlier in life.

An existential coach working with someone preparing for retirement would be aware of the impact the change would have on all the existential dimensions. In the **Mitwelt** or social arena, there is likely to be significant change. The retiree is no longer going into work each day and being with colleagues. For some, that may be a relief, but others may have relied on work colleagues for friendships and social companionship. If a retiree has a partner, retirement may bring new challenges to the relationship. A working couple of significantly different ages could have concerns about whether they retire simultaneously or on each reaching a particular age. One person could retire to be at home alone, or to embark on new adventures, travelling to new countries or trying new experiences, while the other continues to work. This may lead to resentment or a psychological moving apart from one another and developing separate social networks. Paradoxically, the opposite can be true, with the retiree needing to develop new joint social networks rather than relying on work to provide them. Osbourne (2012, p. 47) describes the problem which codependency based upon '*the romantic and meta-physical poetic tradition of two 'hearts' merging into one*' can bring. Yalom (1980) uses the analogy of an 'A-frame' building to illustrate the vulnerability of this situation. When one side collapses, the other side goes with it. Of course, often couples benefit from sharing these new experiences and do not need to share their lives all the time.

A common problem in retirement centres on domestic and territorial issues within relationships in the home. There are many jokes about wives struggling to deal with partners who they previously only saw briefly in the evenings and at weekends and who they now experience as 'being under their feet' all day long, interfering with their routine. Barnes and Parry (2004) suggested that retirees and their partners tended to rely upon existing gender identities to promote continuity as well as change during the retirement transition, believing that the use of gender identities is influential on the quality of retirement. I am not sure how well this fits with my own expectations of retirement, as my partner and I do not fulfil gender stereotypes and the increased visibility of nontraditional partnerships and increased gender fluidity may point to the need for new research. Existentially one would need to explore with the client their understanding of their gender role and the impact this may have on their retirement.

Davey and Szinovacz (2004), investigating the effects of the transition to retirement upon the conflict between married couples, found no change in marital conflict. It would be interesting to consider how this fits with figures from the Office of National Statistics, which show an increased number of divorces in those approaching retirement with the over-50 divorce rate increasing for the first time in 10 years, rising by 5.8% in 2016 among opposite-gender couples in comparison to 2015. Davey and Szinovacz did find that when wives continued to work, conflict increased, resulting in a decline in marital quality of life. Possible reasons for this increase might be related to males still seeing themselves as 'breadwinners' or a spousal power struggle. When the retiree has been a leader, then the change in power dynamics may leave them with nowhere to use the power they are accustomed to other than in their domestic environment.

Retirement also impacts the **Umwelt**, the physical dimension. For many years the retiree may have spent a large proportion of their day out of their home. This will have created a particular meaning of 'home' for them. Home may have represented a place of rest, or it may have been a domestic battleground for which work provided a retreat. Now that they may be spending more time in the home, the meaning is likely to shift. They may notice their home environment anew. They may notice things which they hadn't noticed before and may develop a more emotional relationship to the space they live in.

Often, on retirement people choose to move house. Moving from where one has lived and raised a family to a retirement haven in another locality alters the **Umwelt** and can lead to loss in the **Mitwelt** with a new distance from established supportive friendships and social networks. Kahn and Antonucci (1980) liken this to the loss of the 'social convoy' to which a retiree has belonged being abandoned.

As one grows older, the relationship to one's own body (**Umwelt**) alters as physical powers may wane. For someone who has relied on their bodily strength and health in their leadership role, this change in bodily capabilities and appearance can be a major challenge to their self-concept.

In considering the impact for our spiritual world, the **Uberwelt**, retirement causes us to readdress what is meaningful. Without a framework to give our lives purpose and meaning, we can find ourselves falling into an existential depression or drifting aimlessly towards death. We can take heart from Jung's concept of individuation (the process of becoming an individual) with his view that it is only in the later years that we begin to have a real sense of who we are and what is meaningful to each of us as individuals. Existentialists may look to other writers such as Frankl, who saw us as living in an 'existential vacuum' which we must seek to fill with meaning. He believed that this process makes progress as we develop and mature, defining maturity as a clear comprehension and acceptance of one's purpose in life. Both Jung and Frankl saw us as being on a 'hero's journey' with the 'holy grail' being self-acceptance, meaning and actualisation.

In Eastern cultures there is perhaps a better acceptance that later life provides the opportunity for individuation and search for meaning. There is more time and freedom to indulge in what Tillich (1952) called the 'freedom to be an individual' now that its antithesis, the 'freedom to be a part of', is lessened. This dichotomy stems from Heidegger's original concept of 'thrownness', a term he used to describe the fact that human beings do not choose their parents or the environment into which they are born. As a result, persons are simultaneously members of a community and also individuals. Communities can suppress their members in ways that inhibit individuality. Our work may become our most dominant community.

Many leaders discover that they have looked to work for community and for most of their meaning. They may have given meaning to status and the amount of money they earned, and these are no longer so readily available. Work may have afforded safety and a way of avoiding existential anxiety and uncertainty. Now they must face it full on. If retirees are willing to face the fact that they are entering the latter stages of life, they may wish to acknowledge their mortality as motivation to complete tasks that may have lain dormant. This work can start before retirement, however; Anderson, Burkhauser, and Quinn (1986) found that less than two-thirds of workers retired within a year of their proposed retirement date, suggesting the presence of some apprehension about the ultimate step into retirement. This can be mirrored in the small numbers using coaching in preparation for retirement.

In looking at these dimensions we can see that retirement affects how we relate to ourselves, that is, to our **Eigenwelt**. We have to adjust to the self we have in retirement and the meaning we attach to it. Fewer people may be providing us with a mirror through which we see ourselves. In retiring, we have shed labels which may previously have defined us, but which would also undoubtedly have limited us. For some, the loss of this long-time identity structure can be severely traumatising, with some retirees initially experiencing a void in terms of 'what or who am I, now that I am retired?'

We can see that even in a quick overview of the impact of retirement on the existential dimensions, we have touched on key existential themes. The change in our daily way of being-in-the-world calls for a re-examination of what is meaningful. We can no longer hide behind the structure of the working day to avoid the reality of uncertainty. Even when we plan for retirement, there are always potential wild cards that can result in unexpected and undesirable events.

We may view ourselves differently and be viewed by others differently. Not only have retirees left the work structure and environment, but they have entered a new phase of life in which they may have taken on the label 'senior' with its positive and negative connotations. It may bring cheap travel tickets and so on, but it is also a clear signal that one is moving towards death. Of course this is true from the moment we take our first breath, but in retirement, time and temporality are brought more vividly to one's attention. If retirees look old enough, they may experience the stereotype of being assumed to be physically frail, hard of hearing, with poor vision and slow comprehension. Even when this stereotype is the basis for kind assistance, it can be wounding. Objects of this stereotype can feel that they are being prematurely pushed towards advanced old age and death. To move from a leadership role in which one is seen as powerful to one where people experience you as being 'in need' and perhaps less able to make your own choices can be a shock. If retirees enjoyed their careers and experienced them as giving them power, status, satisfaction and safety from existential concerns, they may experience a type of grieving and anger once the initial excitement of retirement has subsided. It is not easy for some retirees to accept that there may be no demand for them to return to the occupational niche they occupied for so long.

Leaders often have more opportunity than others to continue an involvement with work and to be highly valued for their experience and knowledge. They may set up consultancies which given them addition control with the ability to work only where and when they want, on projects which interest them and provide meaning. There is the possibility of a new and vibrant existence, but it has to be built at a time when energy and motivation may be less than they used to be.

Retirement is not alone in providing us with questions about ending and death. These considerations are with us daily, but it does bring them sharply into focus and we are faced with asking – What was my working career for and what do I do now? From an existential perspective, endings in their anticipation and manifestation represent the key frame of reference of making meaning of our lives.

Coaching provides an excellent opportunity to explore the challenges of retirement. The client defines the focus for the work whilst the existential coach remains alert to all the dimensions and themes we have discussed. With one client, Gregory, I could see many of these in play.

Gregory was a leader in a global company. Until recently he had enjoyed his work, with its opportunities for international travel and its healthy paycheque. However, he now recognised that he had been *watching from the side-lines* as his contemporaries either *retired gracefully or died in harness*. He had never given much thought to his own life beyond work – *'I have never had the time to consider it, just too busy...I guess I imagined life after work as an endless round of golf...I love golf...and time to see sport and do things I hadn't had time for. I had always thought it would be something to look forward to'.* However, the nearer his retirement date came, the more anxious he began to feel, and he felt it would be worthwhile engaging in some coaching sessions. I had worked with him before and so we agreed for some sessions to look at this new phase in his working life.

Gregory recognised that his deep anxiety had begun about a year previously when Tom, a younger colleague, had died suddenly from a DVT. Up until this time he could not recall feeling any existential anxiety and was happy to believe that life would just *'go on as it always did'*. He described how he had gone into Tom's office a couple of days after his death and looked at all the papers laid out on the desk with a sick realisation that his colleague had left work one evening with every intention to return and finish his work but *'it had all just ended'*. It has been a great shock to Gregory and put him deeply in touch with his own temporality and the uncertainty of the future. This was new to him. In his leadership post he felt very much in control and confident of what should (and he believed would) happen from one day to the next. Indeed, a large proportion of his day was spent in long-term planning. One of his certainties had been that he would continue to work until the day he retired and then reap the benefits of that work. Yet here he was faced with evidence that this may not necessarily be the case – something unexpected could bring an end to his plans. He also saw that his colleague had proved easily replaceable.

After the initial shock of the death and the funeral, the office had returned to how it had been before, except Tom was no longer there. His work was taken on by others within the team and within a month a new person was sitting at Tom's desk. This brought Gregory face to face with the realisation that he too was replaceable. He had of course known this intellectually, but now he experienced it in his gut and he found the feeling very difficult to bear. He began to wonder just who he was to others and who they were to him. This also brought to question how meaningful all the work was which he had invested his time and energy in for so long.

It brought to his consciousness how much he had invested in the routine, structures, challenges and satisfactions of his job. Outside of work he had invested very little of his time or energy. Although he had been married for over 30 years, when he reflected on this he realised he hardly knew his wife. His social scene had been built around work. He was now fearful that he faced a very lonely and unsatisfying retirement and that the legacy he left behind in work would soon be forgotten, like Tom.

I facilitated his engagement with the authentic emotions and fears he was experiencing and did not try to make him feel better or suggest that things were not as dark as he was experiencing them. Together we met and explored his fears and his sadness.

He came to see work *'as a phase in my life, not a way of defining the importance of my existence'.* This also meant that he came to look on his retirement as a new phase too. It was an ending but also a beginning. What had gone before, what was happening now and what the future might bring needed to be imbued with new meaning.

He had felt his work to be important and to have some long-standing significance, and now he was not so sure. He explored whether it was important for him to leave a legacy in his workplace. Although ultimately he believed it did not matter, he decided to establish an annual prize for the most promising new manager. He chose this because he identified that what he felt most proud of in his leadership was his development of others and he felt this prize would reflect that. In this way he *'bought himself some immortality in the organisation'* and made a statement about what brought him meaning. He knew that in some way this was a denial of an ending but at this stage it was something he needed, and he hoped that as he invested more outside of work it would become less important and other things would take on greater meaning. He knew that he wanted to be remembered and respected for the effort he had put into his work. He also decided that as he had identified the main source of his satisfaction, the development of young managers, he would establish a small business offering business mentoring and training to those entering management, a project he felt passionate about and excited by.

He addressed his fear of the loneliness, which came with the thought of moving away from his work colleagues and spending more time with his wife. Much to the surprise of his wife, Gregory started taking her on dates to the theatre and cinema, trying to *'discover who she is and what she likes'*. This was something he had given very little time to over the years. He discovered that there were still many interests that they shared and also that there were new things they could learn from one another's separate interests. So, both he and his wife began to feel a new energy and excitement in their relationship.

It was important to him that he not be left with a feeling that he had wasted time, but that different phases in life brought different foci. He felt good about what he had achieved and the leadership he had given to the others and to the organisation. He was able to acknowledge both the gains and losses that being focused on work had brought him, but chose not to concentrate on the past. He discovered new interests and meaning away from his work position and sought to have *'an obituary that said more than he was a good worker and leader'*. His values changed to being more focused on *'being a good husband and a man who enjoys living'*. He realised for the first time that he regretted not having children and saw that his new project to develop new young managers addressed some of that loss for him.

So, as we have seen, coaching can help the individual leader look not just at the strategic elements, but also at their existential needs. As reflected on earlier, we all need to feel heard and seen. We seek positive feedback and respect for what we do, no matter how high we might have risen on the leadership ladder. We need to achieve these elements while remaining authentic and true to our own values and beliefs and those of the organisation. Any tensions across values or dimensional needs can be addressed through coaching.

Coaching, training programmes, mentoring and individual reflection all play important parts in developing a leader. Each leader will have a different learning style, which may vary from time to time and depend on what area they wish to focus their development on. Some love the opportunity for quiet, solo reflection and will choose to read and research alone. Others welcome dialogue and the opportunity to develop thinking through Socratic questioning, engaging with one other trusted person or within a group. Yet others will favour more experiential opportunities, perhaps involving role-play or group work. In planning a development programme for oneself, or for others, it is important to bear these preferences in mind, whilst including the possibility of moving beyond the comfort zone and trying something new.

Chapter 7

An existential approach to preventing, managing and resolving conflict

The nature of conflict has fascinated many thinkers and writers throughout time. There isn't space here to cover the different ways influential thinkers have written about conflict; suffice it to say that some, for example, Aristotle, saw conflict as a battle between emotion and logic. Emotions were seen as a negative human attribute, which needed eliminating. For him, logic and reason were kings, and emotions were the slaves which had to be kept in order. The emotional aspects of conflict were relegated to animalistic instincts of little importance other than the need for them to be subjugated, instead of being seen as the entrance to a path of greater understanding of the other and the situational meaning. Others saw conflict as an essential component of change and therefore necessary for survival and development (e.g. Heraclitus, Hegel, Darwin).

By the time we come to the twentieth century, psychoanalysis focused on inner and external conflicts, whilst social scientists were taking a more sociological look at conflict. For writers such as Coser (1913–2003), social conflict was caused by the struggle over limited resources. His main theme was that conflict arises between an 'in' group (us) and an 'out' group (everyone else), and so it may be considered vital to neutralise or eliminate the rival group. We see this being played out continually in the business world. Coser also pointed out that conflict can have a unifying function as it creates strong associations and cohesiveness within the respective groups, a theory which has been used in the creation of many team-building programmes. At the same time, it creates separation and alienation through the identification of the 'other'; those who are not like us, and therefore outside of our group and our concern. When resources are limited, then each group will see themselves as the rightful owners of the resource and be willing to share within their own group, whilst guarding all resources from the 'others'. This dynamic is seen played out in the playground, as well as in international and territorial disputes.

Following on from Coser, Deutsch (1973) embraced conflict, seeing it as something which can be constructive. He posited that parties in a conflict may both be able to gain from the experience, and that it was not necessary that one side 'won' and the other 'lost'. This has come to be referred to as a 'win-win' outcome. This does not indicate an equal material sharing of benefits; it can be win-win in that both sides learn something about themselves and the other and that the mediation proves transformational.

Glasl (2009) presented a conflict escalation model which also emphasised the situational pressures acting upon people involved in a conflict. Rather than looking for the causes in the individuals, the model emphasises how there is an internal logic to conflict relationships, stemming from the failure of 'benign' ways of handling contradictory interests and standpoints. This may lead to a greater awareness of the steps one should take care to avoid if one wants to prevent a conflict from escalating out of control. He identified nine levels through which a conflict may escalate;

- Tension and hardening
- Debates and polemics
- Actions not words
- Images and coalitions
- Loss of faith
- Strategies of threats
- Limited destructive blows
- Total annihilation through fragmentation of the enemy
- Together into the abyss

In Stage 1 we see the beginning of tensions, with the occasional clash of opinions. This is a common occurrence and is not perceived as the start of an inevitable conflict. However, if a conflict should result, the positions become more fundamental. The conflict could have deeper causes.

From there we enter Stage 2 when parties consider strategies to convince the counterparty of their arguments. Differences of opinion lead to a dispute. The parties try to put each other under pressure and think in terms of black and white.

In Stage 3 parties increase the pressure on each other in order to assert their own opinion. Discussions are broken off. Verbal communication ceases, and the conflict is increasingly exacerbated. Any sympathy for the other side disappears.

Next, each side seeks sympathisers for their cause. Believing one has right on one's side, one can denounce the opponent. The issue is no longer important: one has to win the conflict so that the opponent loses.

By Stage 5 any experience of the other side as being 'like them' disappears; the other person becomes an alien or an 'other' and so can be denigrated. By now, the loss of trust is complete. Loss of face means in this sense the loss of moral credibility.

Entry into the 6th stage is heralded with threats aimed at demonstrating power. One threatens, for example, with a *demand* (£10,000) which is enforced by a *sanction* ('otherwise I'll blow up your main building') and underlined by the *potential for sanction* (showing the explosive). The figures decide the credibility of the threat.

The battle intensifies in Stage 7 with attempts to severely damage the opponent. The opponent is no longer regarded as human. The initial desired outcome is replaced, with limited personal loss seen as a gain if the damage to the opponent is greater.

By Stage 8 the aim has become to annihilate the opponent by whatever means. In the final 9th stage personal annihilation is accepted in order to defeat the opponent.

The nature of conflicts can be grouped under four relational headings:

- Interpersonal (between individuals based on differing goals and values)
- Intragroup (occurs within a group or team)
- Intergroup (occurs between two or more teams or groups)
- Interorganisational (managers in one firm may feel another is not behaving ethically)

We can also think of conflict in terms of the central subject of the conflict – data, structural, value, interest and relationships. Or we may define conflicts by which are overtly interpersonal, opposed to those which are more process focused, in that they are concerned with how work gets done. Business leaders are likely to find themselves at the centre of many of these conflicts or be called upon to resolve them. Conflicts are very costly and time consuming for businesses.

Conflicts may appear to be disputes about facts but they are actually about differing perceptions of events, causing parties to perceive their goals as incompatible. This provides a leader who is attempting to resolve a conflict with a creative challenge – how to challenge perceptions and move the parties in dispute from a place of 'stuckness' to a place of creative possibility. One of the main tasks is to identify commonality, usually on values, and to move the parties from seeing the other as the enemy to identifying the dispute itself as a shared enemy impacting negatively on them both. These are primarily psychological tasks.

To prevent or lessen conflict in the early stages we have to be open to listening to the emotional content of each person's narrative without challenging it rather than trying to form a 'logical' judgment about who is right. When in dialogue with each person, it is helpful to try to understand their unique worldview and their existential dimensions. This requires us to respectfully enter their world, temporarily. We need to match the energy they bring to their narrative. We also need to question whether we are using the same language and, if not, then try to find one we both can speak. Some people use stories and metaphors in their narrative and will feel better understood if the listener also uses some of that language. Alternatively, others will want a sharp, clean, businesslike communication style, although underneath that will lie the same emotional and psychological aspects which cannot be ignored.

Professionally and personally we are constantly faced with conflicts. They can destroy relationships and an individual's self-esteem and balance, leaving them feeling blocked and making it difficult for them to progress. When conflicts occur in business they can lead to time-consuming and costly grievance processes, often ending in industrial tribunals. In the United Kingdom, the average cost of defending such cases is approximately £9000 per case, costing the government about £120 million per year.

In *The Art of War*, Sun Tzu counselled us, when in conflict, to *'Build your enemy a golden bridge to retreat across'*. This is a wonderful concept which calls on us to consider what the conflict is really about, what we want out of it, what we need and what psychological elements are at play. If we merely want to see our desired outcome implemented, do we really need to humiliate the person we are in disagreement with, who may, during the period of conflict, take on the mantle of 'alien', 'other' or even 'enemy', or can we afford to build that golden bridge which will allow the other person to maintain their self-esteem and move on from the dispute?

People are generally negative about conflict, yet without conflict there is little to motivate us to change. Why move from the status quo if it is comfortable and conflict free? 'Good' conflict can result in new ideas, better understanding, problem solving, increased creativity and improved performance. Of course, 'bad' conflict can reduce energy, morale, productivity and satisfaction levels.

Leaders will inevitably come into conflict with others and may also be called upon to mediate conflict between their 'followers'. Indeed, leadership and conflict go hand in hand. *'The ability to manage conflict is considered to be a core leadership competence and can help teams to grow and advance. However, conflict management is one of the most difficult soft skills that someone can master and develop'*, (Giotis, 2010 conference paper).

I have heard leadership described as 'a full-contact sport', and it has been suggested that if you cannot, or will not, address conflict in a healthy, productive fashion, you should not be in a leadership role. While you can try and avoid conflict, you cannot escape conflict. In avoiding it, the best you may achieve is to ignore it for a while, but like an ugly boil, it will inevitably erupt elsewhere. It is a fact that conflict in the workplace is unavoidable. The ability to recognise conflict, understand the nature of conflict, and be able to bring a swift resolution to the conflict is the mark of a good leader.

Some of the most common causes of conflict are opposing positions, competitive tensions, power struggles, ego, pride, jealousy, performance discrepancies, compensation issues, just someone having a bad day and so on. Just about anything and everything creates conflict; the reality is that the root of most conflict is relational and born out of poor communication or miscommunication. If we don't feel heard, understood or communicated with, then we feel disrespected and resentful.

Developing effective conflict resolution skills with good communication at the centre is an essential component for building a sustainable business model. Unresolved conflict often results in loss of productivity, the stifling of creativity and the creation of barriers to cooperation and collaboration.

Perhaps most importantly for leaders, the ability to resolve conflict helps to retain employees. Leaders who fail to deal with conflict will eventually see their good talent walk out the door in search of a healthier and safer work environment.

Every conflict offers opportunity to reflect, learn and re-evaluate the status quo. Indeed, conflict is necessary to avoid complacency. If we remain comfortable, why would we chose to move? No movement and not looking to change and improve is the death knell to any business. Hidden within virtually every conflict is the potential for a tremendous teaching and learning opportunity. Where there is disagreement, there is an inherent potential for growth and development. If you're a leader who doesn't leverage conflict for team building and leadership development purposes, you are missing a great opportunity. Divergent positions addressed properly can stimulate innovation and learning in ways that like minds never will. Smart, brave leaders look for the up side in all differing opinions and do not feel that their authority is under threat.

Using an existentially informed psychological approach to leading on conflict will help to bring about a meaningful and potentially creative resolution. Ideally, a leader will develop ways to minimise the possibility of negative conflicts occurring. But when they do, they will know how to manage them, and if necessary how to resolve them.

A psychological response to dealing with conflict

I have already alluded to Sun Tzu, *The Art of War* and his wonderful image of the golden bridge. He wisely also informs us that, '*If you know the enemy and know yourself, you need not fear the result of a hundred battles*' (2009, p. 11). The importance of knowing oneself is often ignored. However, it is essential to know and understand all parties in any conflict. Indeed, '*If you know yourself but not the enemy, for every victory gained you will also suffer a defeat. If you know neither the enemy nor yourself, you will succumb in every battle*' (ibid.).

This means that conflict is always a psychological and inter-relational event. We need something, or someone, to be in conflict with. Even if I am struggling with an inner conflict, the conflict will be between two opposing wants and aspects within myself, and so still relational. In order to work effectively in helping ourselves and others resolve conflict situations, we must understand our own response to conflict. We can start by asking, do I enjoy it; do I provoke it; do I fear it; do I go numb in the face of it; do I run from it; do I ignore it, or do I simply tolerate it? Some people enjoy conflict and the adrenaline rush associated with it, while others will avoid conflict at all costs. These may not be static responses but may depend on context and who is involved in the conflict. I am more likely to get into conflict with someone I care about than I am with someone whom I am not interested in. I want people I like to understand me and so will invest time in trying to be understood even if this provokes disagreement. For myself, it is better to have a disagreement and 'be known' than to not be understood. Of course, for others the opposite is true. They will not risk disagreeing with those they care about, for fear of anger, rejection or abandonment.

Conflict is always psychological. There would be no conflict if the event hadn't distressed us in some way. If conflicts were purely logical, they would be easily solved as there would be a rational answer which everyone could see as **the only logical** outcome. The truth is, conflicts are never logical; they are driven by emotions and a desire to protect our dignity and self-esteem. We want to be proved right and our 'opponent' proved wrong.

We all experience events differently. This is very clearly seen in witness reports of the same event. Not only may what we think we saw and heard differ, our reactions will differ, too. One person can find the same event devastating, whilst another can find it funny! It is not the event in itself which is conflictual, but our emotional and psychological response to it. A conflict can never really be about 'the facts'; they do not exist. It can only ever be about different perceptions of the same event, which each person will believe to be '**the facts**', and therefore '**the truth**'. There is little point in spending time trying to establish these mythical facts or truths, as they 'exist' only in the past. Whatever happened, it cannot be changed. All that can be changed are perceptions and attitudes, which in turn may alter any desired outcome.

As everything is about perceptions, our own and others, then Sun Tzu is correct when he wrote that we need to know ourselves, and we need to know our enemies. Our ability to understand, communicate with and influence others requires us to have a very good understanding of ourselves—how we prefer to interact and relate with others, our interpersonal strengths, what motivates or demotivates us and what actually happens to us when we are under stress. We often wrongly assume that we know ourselves, but how often do we stop to reflect and question what we believe we know? I cannot know my enemy if I haven't taken the time to know myself. Personally, I am often surprised at what draws me into conflict. Reflecting on what lies at the core of my response may tell me something I did not know or was choosing to ignore. I need to consider why I believe myself to be right in a particular conflict and what the psychological gains and losses are which are riding on the outcome.

A good place to start to consider conflict is by reflecting on our own individual response to conflict. A way into that exploration is to look briefly at what we understand by the term 'conflict' and by the term 'psychologically informed conflict resolution'. What does conflict mean to you? What feelings does the word evoke in your body? What passes through your thoughts and body when you hear the word 'conflict'?

When I have asked this question of people, the responses can be predictable, with words such as anger, aggression, fear, hostility or a similar set of 'negative' nouns – fight, clash, argument and so on springing to mind. Just the word *conflict* evokes various emotional and physical responses, generally perceived as negative or unpleasant. Most people experience some associated bodily sense reaction; they may feel their blood run more quickly, or they experience a fluttering in the stomach, tightening in the forehead or even weakness in their knees. It may provoke a fight, flight or freeze response in relation to the perceived threat to our truth and our self-esteem. It is difficult to even hear the word without some type of emotional and psychological intuitive reaction. So, conflict is clearly both emotional and psychological.

Any conflict intervention process is a psychological encounter which requires people to examine their motivation, needs, wants, values and beliefs. It may also challenge behaviours. Having said that, not all professional mediators would see the need for their work to be underpinned by a psychological understanding of inter-relational human communication. For some, it is an evaluative process where the mediator considers the relative strengths of each side's argument. For me, mediation is first and foremost a philosophical and psychological process. It stems from a psychological disturbance to the parties' equilibrium, one that is strong enough to prevent a logical working through of the dispute. Of course, for there to be a mediation there must be a recognisable conflict, so it is simplistic to start by considering the process of conflict resolution without first looking at what is generally understood as conflict.

Bringing an existentially informed psychological approach to managing and resolving conflict

Dealing with conflict with psychological and emotional elements driving a dispute calls for a psychological approach. Such an approach emphasises core existential elements, such as the unearthing of the value systems, the use of emotional language and the exploration of the worldviews of the disputants. At the same time it seeks to preserve or even enhance the disputants' self-esteem, through working with the fundamental human psychological needs for identity, security and recognition.

All of this fits within the existential paradigm and therefore is a necessary approach for an existential leader. Strasser and Randolph (2004) base their model of psychological mediation on existential underpinning. They see these elements as present in both disputes and conflicts. *'One of the most important elements of...mediation...is the exploration of the covert reasons for the dispute, as well as the overt. The parties will have developed rigid belief systems as their overall strategy for survival in an uncertain world...'* (p. 27) For Strasser and Randolph, conflicts occur when existential givens are threatened. As humans we all share the need to be heard, valued and respected. We are all emotional beings and develop behaviour patterns which stem from our values and beliefs. Existential thought requires us to engage with the truth of uncertainty and so any kind of evaluative mediation approach would not fit this, as it carries an implication that there is a certain right or wrong, or some argument which is better or worse. The challenge to working in a creative existential way is not to be sidetracked looking for what is right or by pursuing what looks to you to be good outcomes, but instead to creatively engage with and explore the uncertainty, creating a new way forward.

This more positive approach to conflict is accepted as a precursor to growth and change and is also reflected in the work of earlier scholars such as Mindell (1995, p. 241) who challenged us to *'Value trouble. Accept nature. Make peace with war'* and Totton's (2006, p. 36) clarification of therapy's key contributions to this area, *'affirm aggression, support conflict, speak up for competition – while also affirming, supporting and speaking up for the victims of alienated and destructive expressions of these qualities.'* When first faced with these challenges, I struggled – what was being asked of me? I came to understand that I was required to accept that conflict is a natural occurrence and if I tried to smooth the waters I was being disrespectful to the depth of feeling those in conflict were experiencing. An existential approach to conflict requires us to 'be' with it, not to try to stop it. We must seek to understand what the participants are seeing as being at risk and why for them it is something worth fighting for. This may mean allowing the depth of emotion to be visible to me, in my mediating role, and to the other person. I have mediated seemingly intractable disputes where one person exhibiting the full extent of their emotional reaction, be it anger, pain or desolation, has been enough to change the other person's view on the situation. When working with conflict we must not be afraid of emotions, the parties' or our own.

Whatever the dispute is about, it is important to take a phenomenological approach and remember that conflict is always about perceptions, not facts. As conflict is personal and emotional, not cold, rational and impersonal, and it is important that a safe confidential space be provided, so that you can access an in-depth narrative from both people in dispute. Notice and respect need to be given to both the factual and emotional aspects of what is said. People will be concerned if you fail to hear 'their facts', even though the real cause of the dispute will not be factual but about the person's emotional and psychological response to those facts. These emotional reactions lead us to see which of their values or beliefs have been challenged and what assumptions they are making about the other person. This is not discovered through asking questions but by exploring, using the skills of active listening. These skills are the opposite of the closed and directional questions used in litigation to try to solve disputes.

The ultimate goal in conflict resolution is for both parties to resolve the issue between themselves. Disputes often occur because communication has broken down. Communication breaks down when people feel they are not heard, so by demonstrating good listening you are providing a future model of good communication which should reduce future conflict.

Through listening we allow both parties to express their viewpoints, but as a leader, not a mediator, they will look to you to also share their perspective. You hold a responsibility to both parties but also to the organisation and so can never be totally neutral. As leader you need to facilitate the meeting and help them pinpoint the real issue causing conflict. It is likely that much of the power to resolve the conflict, if it involves organisational issues such as communication, concern about specific duties and responsibilities and so on, lies in your hands as leader. If concerns about neutrality make it difficult for either or both parties to trust you, then the role of the leader is to bring in a third-party neutral mediator.

It is important for a leader not to ignore a growing dispute in the hope it will go away. Early recognition of the problem and a commitment to engage with it shows respect to those in dispute. This calls on you to be an authentic and clear leader, picking up the responsibility for ensuring action is taken. It is important to be clear about how the conflict is being managed and what your future expectations are. Don't leave it to people to make assumptions about what is happening.

Working with conflict brings leaders in touch with all the existential elements.

Relatedness

Existentially, the importance of understanding the relational aspects of all conflict is central to resolving the situation. As Weixel-Dixon (2017, p. 20) so eloquently puts it, *'As a given of existence, it is not possible to be totally isolated, nor is it possible to be fused with another person; we stand always in relatedness, in some form'*. There can be no conflict without one person inter-relating with another. Equally, there can be no resolution without working on the relationship between the disputants. Most disputes stem from two people who cannot work things out because of personal animosity. If you like, respect and, most importantly, trust someone, you are usually able to sort out most difficulties.

When we are appointing new staff or moving people into new teams, it is worth considering, at an early stage, how well that person will fit in the organisation and the team. Hiring individuals with excellent interpersonal skills who are a good fit with your organisation's culture will reduce the potential for future conflicts. People can have dramatically different values, communication styles, work styles and personality types and yet complement each other. Equally, those differences can increase the potential for conflict.

Existential leaders work with the knowledge of the central importance of relatedness in all aspects of their leadership functions. To facilitate the development of positive relationships, one challenge is to help employees get to know each other. Leaders may provide opportunities for staff to interact in nonwork activities, as well as on a continuous basis within the working day, addressing some of the needs of the mitwelt. This may involve giving assignments that put staff into contact with people they don't normally interact with, and providing cross-training opportunities. Formal employee involvement programmes such as self-directed work teams and suggestion systems that ask for employee input and reward people for their participation may also be helpful. Research has consistently shown that employee involvement programmes have a positive impact on both individual and organisational performance and reduce the level of conflict.

It may seem obvious, but it is important to be authentic and to treat staff equally and with transparency. Many leaders are accused of preferential treatment, and it is incumbent upon organisational leaders to make sure they are behaving in an egalitarian fashion. Even the appearance of preferential behaviour can create conflict situations. In my coaching and mediation work I have often come across quite heated disputes because a 'benevolent leader' has made a generous gift to one person and not others. Often this is equipment such as the latest mobile phone or laptop. Bonus payments where the criteria for their award are not clear are another common cause of conflict.

Leaders must also be aware of the nature of the relationship they develop with their staff. You may remember from earlier the leader who chose to cook BBQs for his staff when they would have preferred him to be more businesslike and take more time providing a strategic lead. It may not be suitable to be 'one of the guys' socialising on an 'equal' basis. I have had staff tell me that they felt uncomfortable and not able to authentically enjoy social evenings in the presence of their 'boss'. They also drew attention to how uncomfortable and disempowering it felt for the boss to pay for everything and how equally upsetting it was if they felt they had to pay when there was a large discrepancy in salaries. So even socialising holds its challenges for the leader and may lead to conflict which is expressed or hidden.

Of course, people do not just to relate to their work colleagues. Most people have families at home. An existential leader will not ignore this, and an organisation's sensitivity to personal and family needs will be evidenced in its HR procedures, holidays, flextime arrangements etc. To ignore the personal world of a colleague and the tensions of work-life balance can lead to conflict and accusations of inequality.

Uncertainty

It is a challenge to any leader to accept uncertainty. Many of the expectations placed on the shoulders of a leader come from the need for others (as well as the leader) to pretend that things are certain and that if we are clear and skilled, we can know what will happen as a result of our decisions and actions. This has to be partly true because if we hold the view that nothing is certain, no matter how true that view may be, then we are in danger of becoming frozen and unable to move forward in life or business. Leaders can cause conflict by offering things they have no certainty of being able to deliver.

Leaders may also choose to ignore conflicts because they wish to believe in the 'certainty' that they have done everything to prevent conflict, and so it cannot happen.

Authenticity

Mindell stresses the importance of 'authentic communication'. Authenticity and responsibility are at the core of existential thinking and leadership. Authentic communication consists of a willingness to take responsibility for communicating in an authentic and compassionate way, resulting in accountability, transparency and honesty. This requires mutual respect for self and all others, valuing differences and developing an ability and willingness to listen openly. 'Perceived' differences based on assumptions are often the heart of conflict. Often, identifying the commonalities, whilst not overlooking the differences, unlocks a dispute.

If we respect others, and ourselves, then the need to be authentic forms an important core of our communication; we wish to be understood, and to understand the other, so it is important to speak the truth and to encourage the other to do so. In so doing we develop and maintain high self-esteem and hold others in high esteem, working co-operatively towards a 'Win-Win' or a 'Good Enough' solution to any dispute. Authentic open listening can be a challenge to leaders who often feel they are meant to present themselves as invincible and all knowing and so do not wish to hear views which differ from their own.

If I try to mediate between colleagues, I am faced with a challenge to my authenticity. I may like or value one more than the other. I may trust the judgment of one and question that of the other. To mediate such a dispute I must remain authentically open to the possibility of being wrong and so listen with equal openness to both sides.

Time and temporality

'Time is money' is a common statement in business. Many leaders are constantly under time pressure and inhabit a world which is governed by milestones, deadlines and long-term plans. These timelines are considered logical and factual. We need to create a sense of time in order to live our lives in relation to others. Randolph (2016, p. 19) reminds us that people in dispute need reminding of the subjective nature of time, *'that both the past and the future exist only in their perceptions'* and so *'The constant and fixed exploration of past events may therefore be futile'*. In looking to the future, those in conflict *'may have an overly optimistic or unduly pessimistic perception of future possibilities'* (ibid). A leader has to authentically manage these presumptions, offering neither an unrealistically positive resolution or threatening the opposite in an attempt to get the parties to settlement before they are ready.

When working to unlock a dispute, we cannot expect a linear timeline. People need time to build trust in the process and trust in the mediator. At any point this trust can be lost and the process will need to return to the beginning while trust is rebuilt.

Values and beliefs

In understanding a dispute, we must gain insight into the emotional world of each party. In this way we can discover the centrality of the individual's value system. We often feel at our most emotional if our beliefs or values are attacked in some way. The attack may come from others or ourselves (when we find ourselves behaving in ways which go against our beliefs). An attack to our values or beliefs, including what we believe about ourselves, can be the basis for the most painful conflict.

By understanding this we can identify emotional stressors. A too-rigid (or sedimented) adherence to a value may be problematic; for example, if an individual places 'loyalty' high in their value set, they may feel the need to follow the behaviours of their peers or institution, even when they experience those behaviours as destructive or wrong. The workplace is often made up of many tribes or cliques and it is a brave person who stands alone for what they believe in. This can lead to disputes with other colleagues and with the organisation.

The task is not to challenge the values of the individual but to understand how they are being played out within the dispute; to challenge tensions, ambiguities or rigidity and to work towards a settlement which takes account of their values. To ignore these beliefs risks coming to a 'logical' solution in what is essentially an emotional situation. Such a solution may seem a good one to the mediator but is unlikely to be sustained if it does not address the values and emotions of those in dispute.

Emotions

Being openly emotional is not expected of leaders but behaving as though one is a robot does not do leaders any favours either. One cannot be in a dispute without being emotional about it. As a disputant one can be angry, sad, confused but not neutral and unemotional. Even when a person is representing an organisation in a dispute that they were not personally involved in, they will have an emotional reaction to being in that position and will wish to maintain their self-esteem in the process and the outcome.

An existential leader is not looking for a dramatic show of emotions, but an authentic acknowledgment of their existence. If we ignore the emotional aspects we lose a great deal of important information. As stated earlier, emotions are always about something, and by looking to understand the 'something' we learn what is at the heart of the communication. Emotions are like colours on an artist's palette; the more that are openly expressed, the greater the opportunities for a creative solution. An existential leader invites openness and honesty. Clearly if we invite honesty, we must commit to deal respectfully with what we hear, even if we disagree or it is focused on personal criticism which we consider to be unfair.

In business communication where speed is considered of the essence, it is tempting just to listen for the 'facts' and to push quickly for a solution, not wanting to be bothered with 'extraneous' information. This can result in a quick agreement, but it will not address underlying issues or be meaningful to those in the dispute, and so it is likely that the conflict will reoccur under different circumstances.

People often overlook the emotional content because the listener is disturbed by emotions and so attempts to filter them out. This may be due to lack of skill or fear of emotional expression. In understanding a person's emotional stance we gain an entry to their psychological world, helping us to interact more effectively and empathically. Having one's own emotions noted may be a rare luxury which allows an individual to feel heard, leading to a major shift in the dispute, with an individual being more willing to move from a sedimented stance to a more fluid approach.

Meaningfulness

We have seen how the increase in working hours and the decline in traditional spirituality and churchgoing has resulted in the need to find meaning in new ways. Today, more than ever, this meaning is primarily personal, yet people are looking for both communal and individual meaning in the places in which they spend most time. For many, that is in the workplace.

Existential leaders will accept the challenge of understanding their own need for meaning and that of those working for and with them. This will lead to positive steps to make work meaningful, starting with the vision which offers a collective meaning. They will also look to make each individual's tasks meaningful and facilitate a meaningful journey through their time in the organisation. To do this requires an investment of time in getting to know staff. It is often not possible for an overall leader to know everyone working in their organisation, but if the ethos of relatedness and interest in others is shown at the top, this can cascade through all levels of the work hierarchy. This creates an authentically meaningful environment which will encourage new people to join whilst retaining current staff who share the vision. This reduces the causes of conflict, as everyone is clear about and committed to the same values and beliefs.

When conflicts do occur, the leader needs to look for the meaning in the dispute. It is rarely about facts but always about emotions. Too much time is often lost poring over different versions of 'the facts'.

We become emotional when our meaning is at threat. To resolve a conflict, any agreement has to hold personal meaning for all involved. This strengthens the commitment to bide by the agreed-upon outcome.

To put it simply, overall the foremost task for a leader is to create a culture of authentic and open discourse, in line with existential principles. This reduces the possibility of negative conflict as it encourages people to communicate with one another, always checking their understanding of what is being said, rather than closing down the debate too early, assuming they have understood. Such communication is rooted in the respect for 'the other', in holding a genuine curiosity about difference and in welcoming creative challenges which can bring innovative and positive change. Building a structure to develop and strengthen such open communication can be aided by a number of initiatives which leaders can introduce. Thought needs to be given to organisational communication at all levels. You can improve communication within a team or organisation by strategically employing informational and problem-solving meetings and by utilising a diverse range of organisational communication tools. Such tools include face-to-face discussions, email, texting, video conferences, online meetings, bulletin boards (both physical and electronic), voice mail and faxes. All of these modes of communication have the potential to improve communication but also to create conflict. Emails and texts are particularly prone to creating conflict, as they are so easy to misread without any accompanying bodily or verbal cues.

Some organisations choose to put time into creating a better understanding of conflict, with its potential for both negative and positive consequences, by introducing relevant training programmes. You can reduce the negative impact of conflict by helping employees develop the skills they need to successfully resolve the conflicts that occur in their lives. This gives people more confidence in their ability to resolve both personal and professional conflict. It also makes people more effective at addressing minor conflicts as they occur, instead of allowing them to become major distractions. Additionally, as poor communication is often a cause of conflict, communication skills training may also be helpful. Through such training, employees can increase their ability to communicate effectively with a diverse range of individuals and manage the communication problems that are often at the heart of organisational conflict.

An existential communication approach enables people to embark on an existential exploration of others' worldviews. A clash in worldviews, particularly in relation to values and beliefs, can cause deep conflict and feelings of alienation and existential loneliness. Learning to listen openly and patiently is the core skill in conflict resolution.

By listening more actively and openly, we will discover more about how a person really is experiencing their work and their life in general. This can lead to people's stress being identified sooner. People who feel stressed are often suffering internal conflict, and if this is not acknowledged and support given, then there is a danger that this internal conflict will become externalised. Stressed people feel under threat. Threat leads us to fight, flee or freeze in order to protect ourselves, so it is not unusual for stressed people to see threats where they don't exist and respond with verbal or even physical fighting. Early identification and support of staff members under threat reduces the possibility of this type of conflict. Leaders need to be aware and in touch. In this way they should become aware at an early stage if someone seems to be stressed or is finding it difficult to cope. It is the duty of leaders and managers to recognise this, but they are not necessarily skilled, nor may it be appropriate for them to offer individual support themselves. Their role is to signpost the way for the individual to appropriate support services and facilitate the individual's access to those services.

A few organisations have sought to reduce conflict through the introduction of a Restorative Justice (RJ) ethos. Restorative justice is modern language for an ancient idea. It attempts to describe a justice rooted in human dignity, healing and interconnectedness. With origins in aboriginal teachings, faith traditions and straightforward common sense, restorative justice seeks answers to a fundamentally different set of questions than those we have so often adopted in response to harm: Who has been harmed? What are their needs? Whose obligations are these? And how do we collectively work to put things right? Susan Sharpe's (1998) book lists five principles or goals of restorative justice.

• Invite full participation and consensus – involving all concerned in an incident.
• Work towards healing what has been broken – both tangible and intangible.

- Seek direct accountability – people to be held accountable for their actions with appropriate reparation discussed and expected.
- Reintegrate where there has been division – harmful actions often create outcasts, alienation and distrust in the community/organisation. Where possible, help will be given with reintegration and the repair of relationships.
- Strengthen the community and individuals to prevent further harm. It is future-focused. The incident becomes a catalyst for positive change.

RJ principles are often integrated into organisations in a practical way through a process known as restorative human resources (RHR). It calls on staff to use clean and careful communication, to always clarify their understanding and not jump to assumptions. It has its roots in various branches of organisational work and support service practise, including mediation and conflict resolution, organisation development, HR Business Partner practise and personal effectiveness. It focuses on developing HR staff so that they can resolve issues more quickly and effectively than through a formal route. The benefits include reduced workload and paperwork while staff and their managers feel better about themselves. Conflicts, disputes and disciplinary sessions between staff and employer are dealt with before the issue goes through a potentially lengthy and costly official process. With RHR, you put together your own ideas of what constitutes this practise, based on your own expertise and learning (Figure 7.1).

The nature of this practise is in effect a meeting place of what the business needs from you right now, the key relationships and politics that impact your work and the choices you make for yourself and your own development as you go forward. The principles behind the RHR approach include

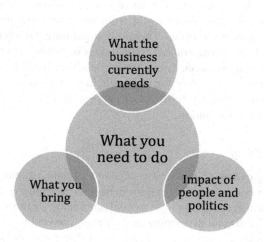

Figure 7.1 Restorative justice business model.

- Giving equal consideration to formal and informal management processes.
- Quick response to possible difficulties. Picking up misunderstandings and poor communication early.
- Addressing underlying issues instead of going for a quick surface fix.
- Introducing, and 'living' restoratively, believing that every relationship has the potential to be improved.
- Developing self-restorative practises aimed at increasing your own well-being.
- Actively owning and managing these formal and informal sources of authority for the sake of the greater good.
- Making time to engage in fuller conversations and going towards what might seem like difficult or awkward topics and situations, often taking an opportune moment to do so, but in a spirit of respect and inquiry.
- Holding and practising the fundamental values of listening, taking responsibility, building trust and embodying respect.

As with existential thinking, RHR accepts uncertainty. It emphasises the inquiry process rather than 'knowing the answer' and works mainly in the third zone of Grint's (2005) types of organisational problems, namely 'critical' (needing a clear chain of command), 'tame' (needing a consistent management of the situation) and 'wicked' (requiring leadership that inquires).

There are a number of themes for the practise of RHR, which link closely with the existential approach. They start with the understanding that we live in an interpreted world, made up of personal perceptions, so everyone experiences the same event differently. They work from the belief that thoughts influence feelings. This, of course, is worth a further debate, but emphasises the importance of emotions. It aims to address needs for reparation for those who consider themselves harmed and to find ways to express their needs and find support for future change.

No matter how hard you work at reducing dysfunctional conflict (conflict that hinders performance and prevents you from achieving organisational goals), sooner or later it is going to occur. Therefore, organisational leaders should also develop ways of dealing with conflict when it does inevitably arise. A conflict can be 'resolved' through litigation, through informal discussion, through physical or emotional violence (bullying) or through using a neutral third party to mediate. A good leader would first try informal discussion, and if that fails then look to conflict coaching and mediation.

Conflict coaching

Conflict coaching can be offered at any stage in a dispute and may also be offered after a resolution is reached if a person's behaviour is regularly causing conflict. Existentially informed coaching can help people communicate in a way which lessens the likelihood of a dispute developing or deepening, or enables the individuals to work their way creatively and thoroughly through a dispute which has become fixed, developing strategies for avoiding and/or dealing with future conflicts.

Coaching provides a valuable tool in helping an individual to identify the nature of the conflict and how to approach it in a creative way. The coach enables and supports the client to manage a specific dispute/conflict, also helping to change individual conflict behaviours and develop general conflict competency. The process aims at enabling the client to develop greater clarity in relation to the dynamics of their conflict and focuses on how they can address and resolve things. The focus of the coaching is shaped by the client's goal, with the coach remaining flexible and alert to the fact that this may change during the work.

The coaching is conducted primarily through explorations which assist the client to clarify and develop their own thinking and understanding of the specific conflict and their relationship with conflict generally. Through the use of effective feedback, challenging and reality testing, the coach then assists the client to identify their options and limitations, to explore the implications of outcomes and to fully consider and take responsibility for their chosen course of action. A key aspect of conflict coaching is for the coach to enable the client to see the importance of understanding and taking account of the 'other' (mutuality). There are at least two people with separate experiences and individual interpretations of the conflict, and of the world. A coach must introduce and maintain the concept of mutuality while retaining a trusting working alliance with the client.

It is this psychological approach with its emphasis on unearthing value systems, emotional language and the worldviews of the disputants that is at the heart of existential conflict coaching. It is challenging to approach conflict in this way within the context of some working environments where 'winning at all costs' is an organisational goal. Often the coach's and/or the client's values may be at odds in such a competitive ethos. The coach has to find a way to work within their own value system whilst acknowledging the worldview of the client and the organisation. The coach must develop a trusting working alliance in which the truth is valued and respected within a context of confidentiality. In some coaching sessions, particularly in the workplace, the coach may find that not only are they working with parties with different identified goals but that these goals may also differ from those of the organisation.

The client may have to make hard decisions. Whatever they decide, they retain the responsibility for the choices they make and need to acknowledge that freedom exists within the existential 'givens'. The coach enables the client to understand their intuitive responses to those givens, enabling them to become creative problem solvers, midwives to their own uniquely meaningful solutions.

Conflict exists where we experience a separation or 'otherness' in relation to other people or in relation to the values and approach of an organisation in which we are 'supposed to belong'. These concepts of uniqueness and otherness may lead to the concept of 'Strangeness' being found in the 'Other'. In a conflict, a disputant often holds a strong sense of the other's 'Otherness' and 'Strangeness', focusing on the perceived differences and thus lacking understanding of the position the other is taking in the dispute. This stems from a lack of understanding of how the other has come to be who s/he is, the values and meaning s/he gives to things and how that contrasts with who they consider themselves to be. In many disputes the parties can see no commonality and yet they may be alike in many ways. They may share beliefs, values and aspirations. A coach will work to identify commonality.

Existential coaching calls for an empathic approach. In order to feel empathy we have first to 'meet' ourselves in the other. It is not easy to feel empathic towards someone or something we experience as alien. In order to facilitate the coaching, the coach has to be aware of the perceived level of difference between participants in a dispute, with all the possibilities this may present for projection and projective identification, and the potential for identification of one of the parties as Jungian 'shadow' or Lacanian 'Other'. If a client learns to approach a conflict with an understanding of their own worldview and those of the other, the meaning each places on the conflict and the commonality or disparity of their values, the work is more likely to focus on issues of emotional reaction, meaningfulness and the importance of values. The role of the coach lies in helping the client to develop a neutral and nonjudgmental stance which considers the meaning and implications, both emotionally and practically, of any conflict and the potential resolution.

The coach helps the client explore the complexity of their place in the world, its limitations, contradictions and possibilities, and to understand the ways in which this is played out in the dispute. The coach may then help the client see that the other party is also approaching the dilemma from their own personal way of being-in-the-world and guarding their own self-esteem.

An existential coach will use the existential givens and dimensions as a framework to help the client explore their own worldview and understand their own and the other's intuitive stance.

In conflict coaching, the client learns to be both a follower and a leader. They come to understand the importance of feeling safe and making those others involved in the dispute also feel safe. The client learns to 'tune in' to the unique world of the other and to hear their story, following, respecting and working with the values, emotions and coping strategies expressed in order to explore their perception of the dispute. Learning to 'tune in' to someone else's viewpoint and not to get dragged in is an important part of emotional resilience. The client has to learn to understand and be sensitive to the perceptions of the other without getting stuck in their newly found mutuality and ignoring what steps need to be taken to address the specific conflict and move towards a resolution. A resolution can only occur when trust has been established and both parties feel they have been respectfully heard.

The coach may work very practically with an individual to help them become more conscious of their own language style and how this may be misinterpreted, leading to conflict. In discovering the client's worldview the coach will also discover what is important and meaningful in the stance the client is taking towards the dispute. This will allow a consideration of the potential gains and losses of any decisions and behaviours the client may choose. The client will clarify what might happen if they choose not to resolve a conflict (e.g. go to court/tribunal, lose their job, their family, their pride, their self-esteem etc.). It is equally creative and sometimes surprising to consider what would happen if they do get exactly what they want, as there may well be losses attached. Getting what they thought they wanted may achieve material gain but fail to bring the emotional state they were hoping for. People are more inclined to be open and creative if they feel they have been listened to with respect. They no longer have to fight their corner because there is no one to fight against – they have been heard and witnessed.

If a leader needs to offer a conflict intervention involving both sides of the dispute, they may choose to try mediation.

Mediation

Mediation is quick. Many mediations are competed in one day. They are also much cheaper than legal alternatives. Unlike court proceedings, mediation offers confidentiality; the only exceptions usually involve child abuse or actual or threatened criminal, violent or dangerous acts. It also offers the potential to come up with very creative solutions (Table 7.1).

The word 'mediation' is used to describe many different kinds of intervention, some in which the mediator evaluates each side's position, some in which the mediator is directive and gives advice and some where the mediator remains neutral and nonjudgmental and acts as a facilitator. An existential approach would only fit congruently with a transformative rather than evaluative model of mediation. Transformative mediation looks at conflict as a crisis in communication and seeks to help resolve the conflict through enabling parties to develop a clearer understanding of their own beliefs, assumptions and needs, together with those of the person they are in conflict with. Sometimes this is couched as helping each side find a way of empathically relating to the other. Of course the mediator also has to find an empathic way of relating to both parties.

Empathy is often misunderstood; it is not about being sympathetic or caring. It is the ability to connect with the emotional experience of someone else and

Table 7.1 Differences between litigation versus mediation

Litigation	Mediation
Can take years	Quick (often just a day)
Expensive	Inexpensive
Binding	Without prejudice until formal signing of agreement
Public	Confidential
Confrontational	Collaborative
Destroys relationships	Preserves relationships
Last resort	Early resolution
Lose/lose	Win/win

so is the opposite of objectifying the other person. Some existentialists prefer the term 'emotional dwelling' to 'empathy', as it carries an active dynamic with it. To 'emotionally dwell', a person needs to cultivate the capacity to enter into another person's reality while simultaneously retaining their own. It recognises the embeddedness of experience in intersubjectivity. So, it is a process which is active and relationally engaged.

Atwood and Stolorow (2016, p. 1) describe 'dwelling' as not merely seeking *'to understand the other's emotional world from the other's perspective. One does that, but much more. In dwelling...and exploring human nature and human existence, one leans into the other's experience and participates in it, with the aid of one's own analogous experiences'.* It is not dissimilar to Freud's 1909 idea of 'evenly hovering attention', first referred to in the case study of Little Hans (Freud, 2001), in which one is alert to the flux of the other's experiences through a kind of floating, open attentiveness, free (as far as possible) from assumptions, preconceptions or goals. Phenomenology holds that our whole experience is filtered through our interpretations, through which we seek to make sense and create our own personal 'meaningful' world. We cannot free ourselves entirely of our prejudices and assumptions; indeed, there are no such things as *immaculate* perceptions, as Nietszche warned us in *Thus Spoke Zarathustra*. One can see that this is not just true for Atwood and Stolorow, writing about a therapist's relationship with a client, but potentially to all relational encounters between human beings.

Existentially informed mediators focus more on needs (both material and psychological) than wants, and importance is placed on safeguarding the self-esteem of all parties. They aim for a solution that is 'good enough', with both parties feeling they have benefited from the process, rather than one party feeling they have 'won' and the other 'lost'.

For mediators taking a transformational approach, psychological understanding lies at the heart of their work and governs their approach. Some mediators do not consider psychological functions when mediating a dispute. They are intent on finding a solution. Psychologically informed mediators start with the belief that every individual is unique, and intercommunication between individuals is innately complex, multidimensional and unpredictable. This is undeniably true in any conflict situation. Despite the fact that a dispute may seem relatively simple in the first instance, a mediator must ask: If that is the case, why has it not resolved without my help? It is rarely the surface issues which keep people in conflict; the more sedimented reasons, often hidden from the conscious awareness of the disputants, are often the causes of prolonged disagreement.

Fortunately one of the existential givens we all share is our need to be heard. This is a gift to a mediator. A common cause of conflict stems from a person not feeling listened to and experienced in the uniqueness of their existence. The mediator aims to develop a trusting relationship with all involved in any mediation. It is these strong working alliances, with respectful and reflective listening at the heart, which can unlock the conflict.

Listening is a lot harder than we may think. As we have read, phenomenologists, drawing on the works of Husserl (1859–1938), base their understanding about how we exist in the world on the premise that objects exist through the meaning that we give. This is known as 'intentionality', which occurs unconsciously.

Husserl saw every act of intentionality as containing two parts; 'noema' which is directional, which is the object (the what) that we direct our attention towards and focus upon', and 'noesis', which is referential, the 'how' through which we define an object. It is important in a dispute that we listen to both the noematic (content) and the noetic (the individual's unique emotional experience of that content) in all narratives. We can only begin to really understand when we listen for and to both aspects. We need to remember that these aspects are interpreted by the individual through the veils of their familial, cultural and individual experiences, including their value sets and emotional context.

There are a number of simple skills which can help to elicit both these aspects. These include the use of encouraging body language, the use of silence, not interrupting, asking open questions, reflecting back, paraphrasing, summarising and the identification of themes which are tracked and deconstructed (rather than analysed). The mediator will feedback any contradictions they hear between noema and noesis, between the values and actions, between the body language and verbal content or any other shifts in approach or outlook. They will explore the assumptions which are being expressed and the emotional context of the statements. To do this effectively, they set aside their own preconceptions and judgments, and listen in an open way. By doing so, they develop greater understanding of the individual's response to the dispute (e.g. emotions, value and belief systems, coping strategies and factors influencing self-esteem), thus helping to understand their fundamental worldview, and facilitate a deeper and more authentic dialogue. Through this dialogue, access is gained to the parties' worldviews, facilitating an understanding of how they are in the world.

Through our being-in-the-world we all develop coping strategies in response to life's challenges. Often these work well, and the individual automatically employs them without being conscious of doing so. They become an automatic response. A common strategy is to choose a position as a 'leader' or a 'follower'. For some, their successful coping strategy is to adopt a leadership position and to forge forward, hopefully taking others with them. Others may adopt a position as follower, preferring not to be in the front line. It does not mean that by taking a follower position one cannot lead. Many good leaders seek out the opinions of others, empower others and lead from the back. Through mediation a person may come to see that rigidly sticking in one role or adopting a sedimented coping behaviour may not serve them well. In mediation, the disputant can see different ways of coping without losing self-esteem. They will gain insight into how coping strategies sometimes work for them but at other times can make things worse.

People in conflict often feel powerless; after all, they have been unable to resolve the conflict themselves and have needed to bring in a mediator. The existential focus on relatedness will mean that the mediator is acutely aware of the need to respectfully honour the importance of their interaction with both parties. The relationship between the different parties and the mediator is built on trust flowing from the authenticity and neutrality of the mediator.

The mediator has to be both a follower and a leader. In the early stages the disputant is the leader, and the mediator follows, slowly unwrapping the meaning of what is being presented. The mediator has to 'tune in' to the unique world of the different individuals and to follow their stories without any judgment. The 'tuning in' process is the central element in building a trusting working alliance with each party, with the requirement to enter into the other's worldview, with its value sets, coping strategies and emotional reactions. The mediation process is neither chronological nor linear. The mediator embraces this uncertainty following where the party takes them. The trusting working alliance may be built and lost a number of times throughout the process.

The mediator will clarify a party's worldview and priorities but will then need to move on to enable the disputant to learn to understand and be sensitive to the perceptions of the other. Having found some new mutuality, the parties need support to identify what steps need to be taken to address the specific conflict and so move towards a resolution. This can only occur when trust has been established and both parties are respectfully heard. They no longer have to fight their corner because there is no one to fight against – they have been heard and witnessed. At this stage the mediator will enable the parties to enter back into the 'world of the dispute' with its concrete and emotional implications, and begin to focus on possible solutions in order to facilitate a 'good enough' solution. This requires a move to the 'tuning out' phase, where the mediator shifts from tuning in to the individual worldviews and draws on the trust which has been created to challenge assumptions, ambivalences and ambiguities. At this stage the mediator may also choose to invite the parties to consider the implications, psychologically, emotionally and financially, of settling or not settling in the mediation.

By employing an existential approach, the mediator improves her chances of gaining a successful and sustainable resolution. If a mediator ignores the emotional and psychological aspects, they may succeed in obtaining a logical solution, but it may be a solution which holds no meaning for the party. When we are in conflict we do not generally act in a logical manner, so a 'logical' solution is unlikely to hold if the more personal underpinning issues are not addressed.

A psychologically informed mediator will seek to maintain or even increase the self-esteem of all those involved in the mediation. At the same time they will haul in their own natural desire to increase their own self-esteem by appearing to know the answers and to hold the solution in their hands. The disputants are always responsible for the solution. The mediator's role is one of facilitation and so they hold the responsibility for the process but not for the content. An existentially informed mediator will not try to rush the parties into a resolution. The process is valued as much as the agreement. It is hoped that the process will not just result in the solution to one point of the dispute but may result in the disputants having a greater understanding of themselves, helping to prevent further conflict.

The structure of mediations can vary. Most start with a premediation meeting or phone calls and the agreement of a premediation contract covering ground rules such as confidentiality, who will attend, fees, venue and so on. In some models, the parties never meet together, whereas in others they remain together throughout and do not have individual private sessions with the mediator. I use the Harvard model, which combines individual sessions with joint sessions.

A leader may feel that they are the perfect person to act as mediator in disputes within their organisation, or they may choose to train an internal mediator, often from the HR department. However, it is hard to see how they really match the requirement to be a third-party neutral, meaning that the disputants may not feel free to speak openly.

As a mediator, I have facilitated many workplace mediations (Hanaway, 2014, 2018) and remain surprised that more leaders do not use mediation early in any dispute. The quickness and the cleanness of the process is beneficial in itself but can also lead to very different but meaningful solutions than the usual litigation and disciplinary routes. I have given a number of detailed accounts of mediations elsewhere (Hanaway, 2014, 2018), so I won't repeat them here, but let me briefly give an example of a situation which was not mediated but would certainly have benefited from the process.

Tania had spent several years in litigation and as a result of the conflict itself and the litigation process she was suffering depression for which she was prescribed antidepressants. She had worked for 14 years in a very stressful job. For 13 years Tania had completed her work successfully and not been the subject of any disciplinary or grievance procedures. One night, after she had been working a 24-hour shift, she lost her temper with one of the clients, and she acknowledged that she did not handle the situation well. She was suspended from work and eventually dismissed. The organisation she worked for failed to carry out the correct process for her dismissal and so began a long legal fight for compensation. Her mental health deteriorated and she knew that even if she was to be reinstated she could no longer handle the stress of the job. Throughout the long, drawn-out legal proceedings, her health worsened to a point where she felt highly anxious most of the time and began to find it difficult to leave the house. Eventually a resolution was reached in which she was awarded a large financial settlement. Her legal team was delighted. However, the client did not feel any better. She put the money in the bank and started therapy.

She explained that the money felt 'dirty' and she did not feel able to use it. She had found the legal process itself to be 'humiliating, bruising and bullying'. I asked her what it was she had needed from the outcome for it to hold meaning for her. Her reply was very simple, *'It was never about money, I wanted someone to say that although I made a mistake, and I never denied that, for 13 years I had done a good job and remained loyal to the organisation'*. If an existential mediator had been employed who had bothered to listen to what was meaningful for Tania, they would have been picked up very easily that some of Tania's existential needs had been ignored. Tania needed some restoration of her self-esteem through an acknowledgment that she had done a good job for a long time. She needed her value of loyalty to have been seen, acknowledged and respected. Overall she needed to be listened to and for attention to be paid to her self-esteem. Through therapy she improved and used the money to retrain.

Whether using informal discussions, conflict coaching or mediation, by paying attention to existential aspects, the person's existential dimensions and an individual's processes of meaning-making, the likelihood of a meaningful and sustainable resolution increases.

Conclusion

Taking a more philosophical approach to management and leadership is not new and is a growth field amongst philosophers and leaders. Amongst those currently working in the field are Koestenbaum, Drucker, Spillane, Flores, Segal and others. Several of these offer case examples in relation to well-known CEOs of global companies. These are fascinating and insightful to read. In this book I have aimed to offer a more personal approach, based more on my own thoughts, feelings, intuitions and experiences, very much aligned to the existential hermeneutic phenomenological tradition. My writing has, however, been influenced by the experience of reading these other writers and my interpretation of what they have to say in their often more objective and academic approach, and I would recommend further reading of these authors if you are left seeking a more academic or research-led view.

I have attempted to move away from business and leadership jargon or what Watson (2003) described as 'assembly-line' language, which he considered to be 'deliberately without any possibility of meaning, emotion or humour'. Such language does not encourage reflective thought. As Heidegger maintained, the function of jargon is to inhibit thought. If I am sat in a room full of people spouting jargon which I do not understand or cannot follow, I feel excluded. It is difficult for me to find a way in. On a good day I can feel sorry for the jargon spouters, as I can recognise it as a defence mechanism. Many people using jargon feel it gives them kudos and that by knowing the language it implies knowledge which they can shield behind, making it difficult for non-jargon speakers to join in, and so limiting any possible lateral challenges which may require the speakers to reconsider their viewpoint. On a bad day the same situation can make me feel small and inadequate. I may want to protect my fragile self-esteem by remaining quiet and not offering any alternative observations or ideas. Neither of those responses makes for a creative collaboration by which two people can learn from one another, and so everyone loses out.

It may be frustrating to the reader that I have also tried to stay away, as much as possible, although not entirely, from writing a handbook full of techniques. To do so would have felt a little like remaining staring at Plato's wall and using the shadows as templates. It may be comfortable staying with what we are taught, but what opportunities and experiences we are missing. Indeed, Kotter (1999) reminds us that managers are not trained for thinking outside the box or for venturing through a cave opening when they are uncertain what they might encounter on the other side. Instead he asserts that people have been raised in a more stable world, and that the leadership training they received was on the understanding this stability would continue. As Kotter points out, this is a world that for the most part no longer exists.

There is no universal or constant set of techniques that will work everywhere and with everyone, yet once we have learnt techniques, particularly those recommended to us by 'gurus', we do tend to stick with them, even though the results may indicate they have ceased to work.

Sartre (1975) speaks of the anguish and resoluteness of engaging intuitively rather than following directives or employing techniques or systems, so I understand the comfort of being given concrete ways to deal with dilemmas. However, such 'instructions' are merely a defence against the existential angst of uncertainty, with the knowledge that there is no true and certain solution to any leadership challenge. What works well for one person, working with one set of people, in one place, may prove disastrous elsewhere, with different people. Despite acknowledging the uncomfortability of there being no certain path, Sartre valued intuition whilst calling for an acceptance that one must make a decision (as choosing not to decide is itself a decision) and thus when one follows intuition, one is choosing freedom, with its attendant responsibility: *'If an intuition speaks to me, it is still myself who must decide whether the (intuition) is or is not a (creative one)'* (1975, p. 31).

As well as offering no techniques, neither do I hold up directives to help the reader become a 'better' leader. Indeed, I would not be able to offer you a definition of a 'better' or 'good' leader outside of the individual's leadership context and knowledge of the team in which that leader operates. All I can offer is an understanding of the existential givens and what they can teach us as leaders. We may then choose to use them as a framework to support innovative thought and reflection.

Moving from philosophers to those experienced in leadership, we do find an understanding of this existential, nondirective approach in the experience of people such as Jack Welch, a CEO of General Electric. He understood the existential journey of a manager or leader to be one in which *'a person commits themselves to a path without support either from other people, from a belief in an absolute such as God and without objective scientific or rational confirmation that we are on the correct path'* (Segal, 2004, p. 107). There is no certainty that there is such a thing as a 'correct' path, but an understanding and acceptance that one must choose a path and follow it with commitment, passion and flexibility. Welch reminds us that, *'...business is smell, feel, and touch as much as or more than numbers'* (ibid., p. 35), jargon or techniques and that if *'we wait for the perfect answer, the world will pass us by'* (ibid.).

This book calls on the reader to choose their path and take ownership of it. May your journey along that path be an interesting, stimulating and exciting one.

Bibliography

Alley, D., & Crimmins, E., 2007, The demography of aging and work, in K.S. Shultz & G.A. Adams (Eds), *Applied Psychology Series. Aging and Work in the 21st Century* (pp. 7–23), Mahwah, NJ: Lawrence Erlbaum Associates Publishers.

Allport, G.W., 1937. *Personality: A Psychological Interpretation.* New York: Henry Holt & Co.

Anderson, E., 2019, From existential alterity to ethical reciprocity: Beauvoir's alternative to Levinas, *Continental Philosophy Review*, 1–19, https://philpapers.org/rec/ANDFEA-5

Anderson, K.H., Burkhauser, R.W., & Quinn, J.F., 1986, Do retirement dreams come true? The effect of unanticipated events on retirement plans, *Industrial and Labour Relations Revue*, 39, 518–526.

Aristotle, 1984, *The Politics*, Translated and with an introduction by Carnes Lord. Chicago: University of Chicago Press.

Atwood, G.E., & Stolorow R.D., 2016, Walking the tightrope of emotional dwelling, *Psychoanalytic Dialogues*, 26, 102–107, doi:10.1080/10481885.2016.1123525

Barnes, H., & Parry J., 2004, Renegotiating identity and relationships: Men and women's adjustments to retirement, *Ageing and Society*, 24 (2), doi:10.1017/S0144686X0300148X

Beehr, T.A., & Bennett, M.M., 2007, Examining retirement from a multi-level perspective, in K.S. Shultz & G.A. Adams (Eds), *Applied Psychology Series. Aging and Work in the 21st Century* (pp. 277–302). Mahwah, NJ: Lawrence Erlbaum Associates Publishers.

Bennis, W.G., & Nanus B., 1997, *Leaders: Strategies for Taking Charge*, New York City: Harper Business.

Blair, S., & Rillo M., 2016, *Serious Work: How to Facilitate Lego Serious Play Meetings and Workshops.* London: ProMeet.

Blake, R., & Mouton J., 1964, *The Managerial Grid: The Key to Leadership Excellence.* Houston: Gulf Publishing Co.

Blits, J., 1989, Self knowledge and the modern mode of learning, *Educational Theory*, 39 (4), University of Illinois: Wiley Online Library, doi:10.1111/j.1741-5446.1989.00293.x

Bloom, A.D., trans. 1968, *The Republic of Plato*, UK: AbleBooks.

Boleman, G., & Deal T.E., 2003, *Reframing Organisations: Artistry, Choice and Leadership*, San Francisco, CA: Jossey-Bass.

Boss, M., 1636, *Existential Foundations of Medicine and Psychology*, Jason Aronson.

Boyatzis, R., & McKee A., 2005, *Resonant Leadership: Renewing Yourself and Connecting with Others through Mindfulness, Hope and Compassion*, Harvard Business School Press.

Buber, M., 2008, *I and Thou*, 1st Touchstone edition, New York City: Simon & Schuster.

Bugental, J.F.T., 1992, *The Art of The Psychotherapist: How to Develop the Skills That Take Psychotherapy beyond Science*, London: W.W Norton & Co.

Bugental, J.F.T., & Bracke, P.E., 1992, The future of existential-humanistic psychotherapy. *Psychotherapy: Theory, Research, Practice, Training*, 29 (1), 28–33.

Carroll, S., 2016, *The Big Picture: On the Origins of Life, Meaning and the Universe Itself*, London: Oneworld Publications.

Caruso, G., & Flanagan O. (Eds), 2018, *Neuroexistentialism – Meaning, Morals, and Purpose in Neuroscience*, Oxford: Oxford University Press.

Cerulo, K., 2006, *Never Saw It Coming: Cultural Challenges to Envisioning The Worst*, Chicago: University of Chicago Press.

de Cieri & Kramar R., 2002, *Human Resource Management in Australia: Strategy, People, Performance*, New York City: McGraw-Hill Higher Education.

Clark, T.W., 2016, *Naturalism and Well-Being. Religion: Beyond Religion (Macmillan Interdisciplinary Handbooks)*, 1st edition. Phil Zuckerberg. London: Macmillan.

Cooper, S., 2012, *Make more money by making your employees happy*, www.forbes.com/sites/stevecooper/2012/07/30

Coser, L., 2011, *The Functions of Social Conflict*, London: Routledge.

Covey, S.R., 2004, *The 7 Habits of Highly Effective People: Powerful Lessons in Personal Change*, New York: Free Press, Simon & Schuster.

Cox, G., 2009, *How to Be an Existentialist: or How to Get Real, Get a Grip and Stop Making Excuses*, London: Bloomsbury.

Dalal, F., 2018, *CBT: The Cognitive Behavioural Tsunami: Managerialism, Politics and the Corruptions of Science*, New York: Routledge.

Darth, W.H., & Palus C.J., 1994, *Leadership as Meaning-Making in a Community of Practice*, CCL Report No. 156, North Carolina: Center for Creative Leadership.

Davis, E., & Miller, D., 1967, *The Philosophic Process in Physical Education*. Philadelphia: Lea and Febiger.

Davey, A., & Szinovacz M.E., 2004, Dimensions of Marital Quality and Retirement, *Sage Journal of Family Issues*, doi:10.1177/0192513X03257698

Day, D.V., 2001, Leadership Development: A review in context, *Leadership Quarterly*, 11 (4): 581–613.

Deal, T.E., 2003. in Davies B., *The Essentials of School Leadership*, London: Sage.

Deal, T.E., & Peterson K., 1999, *Shaping School Culture*, San Francisco, CA: Jossey-Bass.

van Deurzen, E., & Hanaway M. (Eds), 2012, *Existential Perspectives on Coaching*, London: Palgrave McMillan.

Deutsch, M., 1973, *The Resolution of Conflict: Constructive and Destructive Processes*, New Haven, CT: Yale University Press.

Deutsch, M., 2009, *The Resolution of Conflict: Constructive and Destructive Processes*, New Haven & London: Yale University Press.

Dobson, P., Starkey K., & Richards J., 2009, *Strategic Management: Issues and Cases*, New York: John Wiley & Sons.

Drath, W., & Palus, C., 1994, *Making Common Sense: Leadership as Meaning-Making in a Community of Practice*, Greensboro, NC: Center for Creative Leadership.

Dru, J., 1996, *Overturning Conventions and Shaking Up the Market Place*, New York: John Wiley & Sons.

Drucker, P., 1997, *Managing in a Time of Great Change*, Oxford: Butterworth-Heinemann.

Ekerdt, D.J., 2010, Frontiers of research on work and retirement, *Journal of Gerontology: Social Sciences*, 65B, 69–80.

Erickson, R.J., 1995, The importance of authenticity for self and society, *Symbolic Interaction*, 18 (2), 121–144.

Featherstone, E., Interview with Richard Reed in *The Guardian (20.03.17)*.

Flores, F., & Letelier M., 2013, *Conversations for Action and Collected Essays: Instilling a Culture of Commitment in Working Relationships*, CreateSpace Independent Publishing Platform.

Foster, R., & Kaplan S., 2001, *Creative Destruction: Why Companies That Are Built to Last Underperform the Market and How to Successfully Transform Them*, New York: Crown Business.

Frankl, V.E., 2003, *Man's Search for Meaning*, China: Xinhua Publishing House.

Freud, S., 1912, *Recommendation to Physicians Practicing Psychoanalysis, Standard edition*, 7, 109–120. London: Hogarth Press, 1958.

Freud, 2001, *Complete Works of Sigmund Freud, Volume 10: Two Case Histories (Little Hans and the Rat Man)*, London: Vintage.

Gadamer, H.G., 1991, *Truth and Method*, 2nd edition, New York: Crossroads.

Garvey, B., Stokes P., & Megginson D., 2008, *Coaching and Mentoring: Theory and Practice*, London: Sage.

Gazzinga, M.S., 2012, *Free Will Is an Illusion, but You're Still Responsible for Your Actions*, https://www.chronicle.com/article/Michael-S-Gazzaniga-Free/131167

George, B., 2004, *Authentic Leadership: Rediscovering the Secrets to Creating Lasting Value*, Hoboken, New Jersey: John Wiley & Sons.

Gibbons, M., 2007, *A Review of Employment Dispute Resolution in Great Britain*, London: Dti.

Giddens, A., 1999, Globalisation (lecture 1), in Reith lectures 1999, http://news.bbc.co.uk/hi/english/static/events/reith_99/default.htm

Giotis, T.C., 2010, *Leadership through conflict: grow and advance project teams!* Paper presented at PMI Global Congress 2010—EMEA, Milan, Italy. Newtown Square, PA: Project Management Institute.

Glasl, F., 2009, Konfliktmanagement. Ein Handbuch für Führungskräfte, Beraterinnen und Berater, Bern: Haupt.

Goldmark, P., 2002, We are all minorities now, in *Alfred Herrhausen Society for International Dialogue, The End of Tolerance?* (pp. 53–59) London: Nicolas Brealey Publishing.

Goleman, D., 1995, *Emotional Intelligence*, New York: Bantam Books.

Goleman, D., 1995, *Working with Emotional Intelligence*, London: Bloomsbury.

Grant, A., 2016, in *Psychology Today*, https://www.psychologytoday.com/gb/blog/happiness-and-the-pursuit leadership/201606/is-be-yourself-bad-advice

Greenleaf, R., 1977, *Servant Leadership: A Journey into the Nature of Legitimate Power and Greatness*, Mahwah, New Jersey: Paulist Press.

Greenspan, S.I., 1989, Emotional intelligence, in Field K., Cohler B.J., & Wool G., eds. *Learning and Education: Psychoanalytic Perspectives*, Madison, CT: International Universities Press.

Grint, K., 1995, *Management: A Sociological Introduction*, Oxford: Blackwell Publications.

Grint, K., 2005, Problems, problems, problems: The social construction of 'leadership, *Human Relations*, 58 (11), 1467–1494.

Hanaway, M., 2014, *Tales of Conflict and the Role of Mediation*, Henley: The CH Group.

Hanaway, M., 2018, *Existential Coaching Skills: The Handbook*, 2nd edition, Henley: The CH Group.

Hanaway, M., 2018, *Musical Differences: Mediating Conflict in the Music Industry*, Henley: The CH Group.

Hanaway, M., 2019, *The Existential Leader*, Abingdon: Routledge.

Hanaway, M., & Reed J., 2012. *Existential Coaching Skills: The Handbook*, Henley: The CH group.

Heidegger, M., 1962, *Being and Time*, trans. Macquarrie J. & Robinson E., Oxford: Blackwell.

Held, D., McGrew A., Goldblatt D., & Perraton H., 1999, *Global Transformations*, Stanford CA: Stanford University Press.

Husserl, E., 2009, *The Basic Problems of Phenomenology: From the Lectures, Winter Semester, 1910–1911*, New edition, trans. Farin I., & Hart J.G., New York City: Springer.

Ibarra, H., 2015, The authenticity paradox, *Harward Business Review*, 93, 52–59. https://hbr.org/2015/01/the-authenticity-paradox

Jacobs, Y., 2019, *An Introduction to Existential Coaching: How Philosophy Can Help Your Clients Live with Greater Awareness, Courage and Ownership*, London: Routledge.

Judaken, J., 2008, *Race after Sartre: Antiracism, Africans Existentialism, Postcolonialism*, New York: State University of New York.

Jung, C.G., 2018, *Psychological Types*, Create Space Independent Publishing Platform.

Kahn, R.L., & Antonucci T.C., 1980, Convoys over the life course: Attachment, roles, and social support, In: Baltes, P.B. and Grim, O.G., Eds., *Life Span Development and Behavior*, Vol. 3, New York: Academic Press, 253–286.

Kelly, L., 1998, *An Existential-Systems Approach to Managing Organizations*, Westport, CT: Quorum Books.

Kernis, M., 2003, Towards a conceptualization of optimal self-esteem, *Psychological Inquiry*, 14 (1), 1–26.

Kets de Vries, M.F.R., 2003, *Leaders, Fools and Imposters: Essays on the Psychology of Leadership*, New York: iUniverse Inc.

Kierkegaard, S., 1844 (1980), *The Concept of Anxiety*, trans. Thomte R., Princeton: Princeton University Press.

Kierkegaard, S., 1992, *Concluding Unscientific Postscript to Philosophical Fragments*, Volume 1 (Kierkegaard's Writings, Vol 12.1), trans Hong H.V. & Hong E.H., Princeton University Press.

Kilduff, M., & Tsai W., 2003, *Social Networks and Organizations*, London: Sage.

Koestenbaum, P., 2001, *Freedom and Accountability at Work: Applying Philosophic Insight to the Real World*, New Jersey: John Wiley & Sons.

Kotter, J.P., 1999, *A Force for Change: How Leadership Differs from Management*, New York: Free Press.

Laing, R.D., 1960, *The Divided Self: An Existential Study in Sanity and Madness*, London: Tavistock Publications.

Laing, R.D., 1961, *The Self and Others*. London: Tavistock Publications.

Laing, R.D., & Cooper D.G., 1971, *Reason and Violence*, New York: Pantheon Books.

Leuner, B., 1966, Emotional intelligence and emancipation, *Praxis der Kinderpsychologie und Kinderpsychiatrie*, 15: 193–203.

Likert, R., 1967, *The Human Organization: Its Management and Value*, New York: McGraw-Hill.

Lipman-Blumen J., 2000, *Connective Leadership*, Oxford University Press.

Lowe, J., 1998, 'Neutron Jack Welch,' *San Diego Metropolitan Magazine*, http://www. sandiegometro.com/1998/may/money.html

Lowe, J., 2001, *Jack Welch Speaks: Wisdom from the World's Greatest Business, Leader*, New York City: John Wiley& Sons.

Lyons, D., 2019, *Lab Rats: Why Modern Work Makes People Miserable*, London: Atlantic Books.

Managing Mentors, 2013, *Coaching vs. Mentoring: 25 Ways They're Different. A Thought Paper for Sharing*, Management Mentors.

Marsden, T., & Mooney P., 2006, Conceptualizing rurality, in Cloke P., Marsden T., & Mooney P. (Eds), *The Handbook of Rural Studies*, London: Sage Publications.

McAdams, D., 2009, *The Person: An Introduction to the Science of Personality Psychology*. Hoboken, NJ: Wiley.

McGregor, D., 2006, *The Human Side of Enterprise*, New York: McGraw-Hill Education.

McIntyre, A., 1967, Ontology, in P. Edwards (Ed.), *Encyclopedia of Philosophy*, Vol. 5. London: Collier Macmillan.

Mindell, A., 1995, *Sitting in the Fire*, San Francisco, CA: Deep Democracy Exchange.

Mischel, W., 1968, *Personality and Assessment*, New York: Wiley.

Mischel, W., 2003, *Introduction to Personality: Toward Integration*, 7th edition, New York City: John Wiley & Sons.

Murphy Paul, A., 2010, *The Cult of Personality Testing: How Personality Tests Are Leading Us to Miseducate Our Children, Mismanage Our Companies, and Misunderstand Ourselves*, New edition, New York: Free Press.

Nelson, N.C., 2012, *Make More Money by Making Your Employees Happy*, Malibu, CA: MindLab Publishing.

Nietzsche, F., 1974, *Thus Spoke Zarathustra*, London: Penguin Classics.

Nietzsche, F., 1978, *Thus Spoke Zarathustra*, Harmondsworth: Penguin Books.

Nietzsche, F., 1998, *Twilights of the Idols or How to Philosophize with a Hammer*, Oxford: Oxford University Press.

Oden, H.W., 1999, *Transforming the Organization: A Social-Technical Approach*, Santa Barbara, CA: Praeger.

O'Gorman, F., 2016, *Worrying: A Literary and Cultural History*, Reprint edition, London: Bloomsbury Academic.

Osborne, J.W., 2012, Psychological Effects of the Transition to Retirement (Effets psychologiques de la transition vers la retraite), *Canadian Journal of Counselling and Psychotherapy* 45/Revue canadienne de counseling et de psychothérapie 46. University of Alberta.

Peltier, B., 2009, *The Psychology of Executive Coaching: Theory and Application*, 2nd edition, London: Routledge.

Pfeffer, J., 2015, *Leadership BS: Fixing Workplaces and Careers One Truth at a Time*, New York City: Harper Business.

Porter, E.H., 1971, *Strength Deployment Inventory*. Carlsbad, CA: Personal Strengths Publishing.

Raisel, E.M., 2001, *McKinsey Mind: Understanding and Implementing the Problem-Solving Tools and Management Techniques of the World's Top Strategic Consulting Firm*, McGraw-Hill

Randolph, P., 2016. *The Psychology of Conflict: Mediating Conflict in a Diverse World*, London: Bloomsbury Continuum.

Richardson, T., 2015, *The Responsible Leader*, London: Kogan Page.

Rickards, T., & Clark M., 2006, *Dilemmas of Leadership*, Routledge.

Rothkopf, D., 1997, In Praise of Cultural Imperialism? *Foreign Policy*. 107, 38, doi:10.2307/1149331.

Said, E., 1995, *Orientalism; Western Conceptions of the Orient*. London: Penguin Books.

Salovey, P., & Mayer J., 2004, *Key Readings on the Mayer and Salovey Model*, Natl Professional Resources.

Sanderson, G., 2004, Existentialism, Globalisation and the Cultural Other, *International Education Journal*, 4 (4), 2004 Educational Research Conference 2003 Special Issue, http://iej.cjb.net

Sartre, J.P., 1975, *Existentialism and Humanism*, London: Eyre Methuen Ltd.

Sartre, J.P., 2003, *Being and Nothingness*, 2nd edition, London: Routledge.

Schien, E.H., & Schein P.A., 2018, *Humble Leadership*, Oakland CA: Berrett-Koehler.

Schmitt, N., 2012, *The Oxford Handbook of Personnel Assessment and Selection*, Oxford University Press.

Schultz, K., 2004, *When Work Means Meaning – Existential Dimensions-Organizations and Leadership*, Copenhagen: Hans Reitzels Forlang.

Schumpeter, J.A., 1950, *Capitalism, Socialism, and Democracy*, Glasgow: Harper Collins.

Segal, S., 2005, *Business Feel: From the Science of Management to the Philosophy of Leadership*, New York: Palgrave Macmillan.

Segal, S., 2014, *Business Feel: Leading Paradigm Shifts in Organisations*, New York: Palgrave MacMillan.

Sharpe, S., 1998, *Restorative Justice: A Vision for Healing and Change*, Edmonton Victim Mediation Society.

Shultz, K.S., & Henkens K., 2010, Introduction to the changing nature of retirement: an international perspective, *International Journal of Manpower*, 31 (3), 265–270.

Shultz, K., & Wang M., 2011, *Psychological Perspectives on the Changing Nature of Retirement*, Kenneth S.

Simone, M., 2001, *Beauvoir and the Second Sex: Feminism, Race and the Origins of Existentialism*, Oxford: Rowman & Littlefield.

Smircich, L., & Morgan G., 1982, Leadership: The management of meaning, *Journal of Applied Behavioral Science*, 18 (3), 257–273.

Solomon, R.C., & Fernando F., 2003, *Building Trust in Business, Politics, Relationships and Life*, Oxford University Press.

Spillane, R., 2007, *An Eye for an I: Living Philosophy*, Australia: Michelle Anderson Publishing.

Spinelli, E., 2005, *The Interpreted World: An Introduction to Phenomenological Psychology*, London: Sage.

Spinelli, E., 2007, *Practicing Existential Psychotherapy: The Relational World*, London: Sage.

Strasser, F., 1999, *Emotions*, London: Gerald Duckworth & Co Ltd.

Strasser, F., & Strasser A., 1997, *Existential Time Limited Therapy*, London: Wiley.

Strasser, F., & Randolph P., 2004, *Mediation: A Psychological Insight into Conflict Resolution*, London: Continuum.

Sue, D.W., Arredondo P., & McDavis R.J. 1992. Multicultural counseling competencies and standards: A call to the profession. *Journal of Multicultural Counseling and Development*, 20 (2), 64–88.

Sue, D.W., Bernier, J.E., Durran, A., Feinberg, L., Pedersen, P., Smith, E.J., & Vasquez-Nuttall, E. 1982. Position Paper: Cross-Cultural Counseling Competencies. https://doi.org/10.1177/0011000082102008.

Sun Tzu, 2009, *The Art of War*, Oxford: Pax Librorum (Blackwells).

Szinovacz, M.E., & Davey, A., 2005. Predictors of perceptions of involuntary retirement. *The Gerontologist*, 45 (1), 36–47.

Tillich, P., 1952, *The Courage to Be*. New Haven, CT: Yale University Press.

Totton, N., 2006, *The Politics of Psychotherapy*, Oxford: Oxford University Press.

Tzu, S., 2009, *The Art of War*, Pax Librorum.

Ulrich, D., & Ulrich W., 2010, *The Why of Work: How Great Leaders Build Abundant Organizations That Win*, New York City: McGraw-Hill Professional.

Victor, C., 1994, *Old Age in Modern Society: A Textbook of Social Gerontology*, London: Chapman & Hall.

Watson, G., 2003, *Free Will (Oxford Readings in Philosophy)*, 2nd edition, USA: Oxford University Press.

Weixel-Dixon, K., 2017, *Interpersonal Conflict*, Abingdon, UK: Routledge.

Welch, J., 2001, *Jack*, London: Headline Books Publishing.

Westbam, B., 2002, in Ali M., *The End of Tolerance?* Boston: Nicholas Brearley.

Western, S., 2013, *Leadership: A Critical Text*, London: Sage.

Whitmore, J., 1992. *Coaching for Performance*. London: Nicholas Brealey.

Whyte, W.H., 1956, *The Organisation Man*, First Clarion Paperback edition, New York City: Simon & Schuster.

Yalom, I.D., 1980, *Existential Psychotherapy*, New York: Basic Books.

Yalom, I.D., 2008, *Staring at the Sun: Overcoming the Terror of Death*, San Francisco, CA: Jossey-Bass.

Yarn, D., 1999, *Dictionary of Conflict Resolution*, San Francisco, CA: Jossey-Bass.

Index

Note: **Bold** page number denotes Table. *Italic* page number denotes Figure

'A-frame' analogy 107
Anderson, E. 26
Antonucci, T.C. 107
anxiety 9
Aristotle 113
Arredondo, P. 27
'assembly-line' language 137
assets of company, intangible 19
attention, evenly hovering 132
Atwood, G.E. 132
Authentic Leadership 35
authenticity 122–123; *see also* existential
    approach to conflict
'aware self' 8

Beehr, T.A. 106
'being' 7
beliefs 10
Bennett, M.M. 106
Bernier, J.E. 27
boredom 68
Boyatzis, R. 23
Bracke, P.E. 50
brain evolution 11
Buber, M. 50
Bugental, J.F.T. 50
business colour designations 62–63

Caruso, G. 10
CBT *see* cognitive behavioural therapy
Cerulo, K. 10
charismatic leader 17; *see also* leader
Clark, M. 22
Clark, T.W. 11, 22
coaches 83

coaching 77, 84; vs. mentoring 78, **79–82**;
    see also existential coaching
cognitive behavioural therapy (CBT)
    73–74
colour designations, business 62–63
communicating vision 57; revisiting and
    deconstructing vision 58–59; *see also*
    vision
communication 120; *see also* existential
    approach to conflict
company's intangible assets 19
Concluding Unscientific Postscript 95
conflict 113; causes of 116; coaching
    128–131; escalation model 114–115;
    about facts 115; leadership and 116;
    merits of having 117; nature of 115; *see
    also* existential approach to conflict
Connective Leadership 22
convention-disruption-vision 44; *see also*
    vision
corporate life 43
Coser, L. 113
CREATE 90, 91, *92*
creative destruction 44; *see also* vision
Cult of Personality Testing, The 62
Cultural Other 28

Davey, A. 107
defamiliarization 44–45; *see also* vision
destruction, creative 44; *see also* vision
Deutsch, M. 113
dimensions of human existence 85
diversity 27
Dobson, P. 59
Drath, W. 31

Dru, J. 44
Drucker, P. 43, 44
Durran, A. 27

EAPs *see* Employee Assistance Programmes
EI *see* Emotional Intelligence
Ekerdt, D.J. 105
emotional being 37–39; *see also* existential challenges of leadership
emotional dwelling 132
Emotional Intelligence (EI) 22
emotions 8, 113, 124; suppressed 38; *see also* existential approach to conflict
Employee Assistance Programmes (EAPs) 73
emptiness 68
EQ *see* Emotional Intelligence
Erickson, R.J. 9
existence, temporal 29–30
existential 7; anxiety 9, 21; challenge 8; death and uncertainty 8–9; dimensions 12, 106; givens 32; leader 19; meaning of life 11; psychotherapy 86–89; sensitivity to individual worldviews 19; thinkers 26; uncertainty 15; vision statement 47–48; *see also* Hanaway existential dimension
existential approach 61; to create vision 48; existential vision statement 47–48; leader vs. leadership development 74; in recruitment 61–66; in retaining staff 67–74; in staff development 74–84; value-led examples 49–57; in vision execution 43–46; *see also* existential coaching; vision
existential approach to conflict 113; authenticity 122–123; communication 120; conflict coaching 128–131; conflict resolution goal 120; emotions 124; intentionality 133; litigation vs. mediation **131**; meaningfulness 125; mediation 131–136; mediators 132–136; noema and noesis 133; psychological approach 119–121; psychological response 117; relatedness 121–122; restorative justice 126–**127**; RHR approach 127–128; time and temporality 123; uncertainty 122; values and beliefs 123–124; *see also* conflict

existential challenges of leadership 25; authenticity 35–36; cultural competency 27; diversity at leadership level 27; emotional being 37–39; freedom 36–37; meaning-making 30–32; Otherness 26; relatedness 25–29; *supposedly stable binary opposition* 28; task to meaning oriented business 31; temporality 29–30; uncertainty 34–35; values and beliefs 32–34
existential coaching 74, 83, 130; aim 84–85; analogy of 'A-frame' 107; behaving authentically 102–103; coach and client 97; CREATE model 90, 91, *92*; for director of global company 105; existential dimensions 85, 97–101; existential themes in leadership 87–88; GROW model 84, 89, **90**; guidelines for 94; in leader development 111–112; MOVER model 90, 92–94, *93*; and psychotherapy 86–89; recognising existential needs 109–111; re-examining values and emotions 101; retirement challenge 105–109; *see also* existential approach; leadership
existential leadership 5, 25; existential themes in 87–88; programmes 76; working practically with 41
existential psychologists and psychometric testing 65
existentialism 7, 12; Caruso and Flanagan 11; neuroscience and 10
existentialists 7; 'aware self' 8; criticisms 8; throwness 10

Featherstone, E. 57
Feinberg, L. 27
Fernando, F. 23
FIRO-B *see* Fundamental Interpersonal Relations Orientation-Behaviour
Flanagan, O. 10
Flores, F. 31, 44
Foster, R. 44
Frankl, V.E. 45, 108
freedom 36–37; *see also* existential challenges of leadership
Freud, S. 132
Fundamental Interpersonal Relations Orientation-Behaviour (FIRO-B) 65

Garvey, B. 84
Gazzinga, M.S. 11

Giddens, A. 20
Giotis, T.C. 116
Glasl, F. 114
global me 20
globalisation 20–21
Goldblatt, D. 20
Goldmark, P. 20
Grant, A. 23
Grint, K. 44
GROW model 84, 89, **90**

Hanaway existential dimensions 12, *13*;
    see also existential
Hanaway, M. 16, 65, 86
Heidegger, M. 8, 9, 26, 41, 50, 58, 68,
    83, 137
Held, D. 20
Henkens, K. 106
human existence dimensions 85
humble leadership 24
Husserl, E. 7, 8, 23, 83, 133

Ibarra, H. 23
intentionality 83, 133

jargon 137
Judaken, J. 26, 27
Jung, C.G. 62, 108

Kahn, R.L. 107
Kaplan, S. 44
Kelly, L. 43
Kernis, M. 23, 103
Kets de Vries, M.F.R. 32
Kierkegaard, S. 7, 9, 36, 41, 83
Kilduff, M. 23
Koestenbaum, P. 137
Kotter, J.P. 138

leader 15; charismatic 17; development
    74; existential fears of 16; illusional
    certainty of future 15–16; need for 15;
    quiet 17; requirements of 16; resonant 23;
    responsible 23–24; servant 17; vision 43
leaderless resistance 15
leadership 95; and conflict 116;
    development 74; Existential Leadership
    programmes 76; stages of careers in
    96; strategic 103; styles 16–17; theories
    45; transactional 16; transformational
    16; uncertainty 96; *see also* existential
    coaching

leadership for, 21st century 19, authenticity
    23, 35; challenges 19–24; connective 22;
    existential leader 19; globalisation 20–
    21; humble 24; management of meaning
    22; new approaches 22; participative
    consultations 19–20; Resonant leader
    23; responsible leaders 23–24
Lego Serious Play (LSP) 75
Letelier, M. 31, 44
Likert, R. 16
Lipman-Blumen, J. 22
living authentically 8–9
Lowe, J. 22
LSP *see* Lego Serious Play
Lyons, D. 70, 75

Management Mentors 78, **79–82**
Managerial Grid 17
MBTI *see* Myers-Briggs Type Indicator
McDavis, R.J. 27
McGregor, D. 17
McGrew, A. 20
McIntyre, A. 8
McKee, A. 23
meaning: of life 11, 45; makers 31;
    -making 30–32; *see also* existential
    challenges of leadership
meaningfulness 125; *see also* existential
    approach to conflict
mediation 131–136; *see also* existential
    approach to conflict
mediators 132–136
mentor 77
mentoring 77; vs. coaching 78, **79–82**;
    see also existential coaching
Mindell, A. 120, 122
Mischel, W. 65
Morgan, G. 22
MOVER 90, 92–94, *93*
Murphy Paul, A. 62
Myers-Briggs Type Indicator (MBTI) 62

naturalism 10
negative emotions 7
neuroexistentialism 10
Nietzsche, F. 7, 30, 41

O'Gorman, F. 10
optimistic bias 10
organisational behaviour frames 12
Osborne, J.W. 106
Otherness 26, 129

Palus, C. 31
Pedersen, P. 27
Peltier, B. 94, 95
Perraton, H. 20
personality: psychology 65; tests 63;
   theory 62–63
Pfeffer, J. 23
phantom cell structure 15; *see also* leader
phenomenologists 7
phenomenology 83, 132
physical dimension 12, 13; *see also*
   existential
Plato's cave 43
Porter, E.H. 62
psychological dimension 12, 13; *see also*
   existential
psychology, personality 65
psychometrics 61–62

Q&A *see* Questions and Answer
Questions and Answer (Q&A) 58
quiet leader 17; *see also* leader

race as social construct 26
Randolph, P. 119, 123
rationality 7
recruitment 61; behaviour and values 66;
   grouping people 62;
   Myers-Briggs Type Indicator 62;
   psychometrics 61–62; use of personality
   tests for 63–65
Reed, J. 86
relatedness 25–29, 121–122; *see also*
   existential approach to conflict;
   existential challenges of leadership
Resonant leader 23
responsible leaders 23–24
restorative human resources (RHR)
   127, 128
Restorative Justice (RJ) 126–127; business
   model **127**
retention 67; boredom 68–69; CBT
   73–74; communication 71; experience
   of belonging 71–72; mentorship 72;
   reasons for leaving 67; relatedness to
   existential thought 73; reward scheme
   69–70
retirement 105–109
RHR *see* restorative human resources
Richards, J. 59
Richardson, T. 23, 24
Rickards, T. 22

RJ *see* Restorative Justice
runaway world 20

Said, E. 28
Sanderson, G. 8, 20, 28
Sartre, J.P. 7, 9, 26, 41, 73, 83, 103, 138
Schmitt, N. 65
Schultz, K. 30, 33, 34
Schumpeter, J.A. 44
Schumpeter's gale *see* creative destruction
Segal, S. 31, 43, 61, 137
servant leaders 17; *see also* leader
shared values 48
Shultz, K.S. 106
Smircich, L. 22
Smith, E.J. 27
social: conflict 113; dimension 12, 13
Solomon, R.C. 7, 23
Spillane, R. 137
Spinelli, E. 10, 94, 101
spirituality 12, 13, 45; *see also* existential
staff development 74–84
Starkey, K. 59
Stolorow, R.D. 132
Strangeness 129
Strasser, A. 97
Strasser, F. 97, 101, 119
Sue, D.W. 27
Sun Tzu 116, 117, 118
supposedly stable binary opposition 28
suppressed emotions 38
Szinovacz, M.E. 107

temporal existence 29–30
temporality 29–30; *see also* existential
   challenges of leadership
therapeutic workplace coaching 86
throwness 10, 108
Tillich, P. 8, 108
time and temporality 123; *see also*
   existential approach to conflict
training programmes 77
transactional leadership 16; *see also*
   leader
transformational leadership 16; *see also*
   leader
Tsai, W. 23
Tzu, S. 116, 117, 118

übermensch 11
Ulrich, D. 31
Ulrich, W. 31

uncertainty 9, 34–35, 122; *see also*
    existential approach to conflict;
    existential challenges of leadership

values: and beliefs 32–34, 123–124; shared
    48; *see also* existential approach to
    conflict
van Deurzen, E. 65
Vasquez-Nuttall, E. 27
vision 41–42; communicating
    57–59; convention-disruption-
    vision 44; creative destruction 44;
    defamiliarization 44–45; existential
    approach to 43–46; Heidegger's process
    of 'destruction' 44; leader 43; meaning
    55; Plato's cave 43
vision statements of companies 55;
    anxiety 55; being commercial 53; being
    entrepreneurial 52; being generous 53;
    being ourselves 52; being present for
    customers 51; being responsible 52;

creating memories 50–51; evaluate
    choices 56; existential elements 47–48,
    53, 54; models for 48; opportunities
    55–56; relatedness 54; responsibility
    51–52, 55, 56–57; uncertainty 55;
    values and beliefs 49, 56; working as
    one team 51

Watson, G. 137
Weixel-Dixon, K. 121
Welch, J. 22, 59, 138
Westbam, B. 28
Western, S. 78
Whitmore, J. 84, 89
Whyte, W.H. 63
work 45
workplaces 46

X and Y theory 17

Yalom, I.D. 9, 107

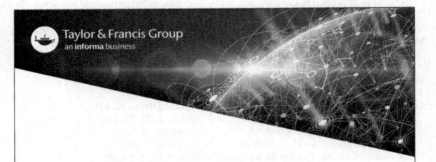